PARISH OF
ST THOMAS, SOMERCOTES

Service of

Remembrance

THEY SHALL GROW NOT OLD

THEY SHALL GROW NOT OLD

Liturgies for Remembrance

Brian Elliott CF

authorized and commended services
for use principally in the British Isles and Commonwealth,
with extra resources and worked examples

CANTERBURY PRESS
Norwich

Compilation copyright © Brian Elliott CF 2006

First published in 2006 by the Canterbury Press Norwich
(a publishing imprint of Hymns Ancient & Modern Limited,
a registered charity)
9–17 St Alban's Place, London N1 0NX

www.scm-canterburypress.co.uk

The poppy illustration is used by permission of
the Florida Center for Instructional Technology

British Library Cataloguing in Publication data

A catalogue record for this book is available
from the British Library

ISBN-10: 1 85311 745 5
ISBN-13: 978 1 85311 745 9

Cover design by Leigh Hurlock

Designed by Simon Kershaw
and typeset in Perpetua
at crucix www.crucix.com

Printed and bound in Great Britain
by MPG Books Ltd

To my colleagues in
the Royal Army Chaplains' Department

and my fellow chaplains
in the Royal Navy and Royal Air Force;

to those who served in two world wars
and in subsequent operations
around the world;

and to those who are currently
ministering to servicemen and women in
dangerous and challenging circumstances.

Blessed God,
who has committed the glorious Gospel to our trust,
have mercy upon the Royal Army Chaplains' Department;
and grant that we may never glory
save in the Cross of our Lord Jesus Christ;
but in all things may approve ourselves as your ministers;
through the same your Son Jesus Christ our Lord. Amen.

The Collect of the Royal Army Chaplains' Department

CONTENTS

FOREWORD

by the Dean of Windsor and Bishop to Her Majesty's Forces

For much of the twentieth century, a significant proportion of the population had personal memories of the First or the Second World War. The eleventh of November, or the nearest Sunday, were times of national remembrance observed by a huge number of people who, in silence, remembered those of their families and friends who had died in those two costly conflicts. They remembered too their own experiences of war, whether as members of the armed services or as civilians.

As the century drew to a close, inevitably fewer people had had first-hand experience of either of the two World Wars. However, as chaplains frequently remind recruits in the armed services, there has only been one year since the end of World War II in which no sailor, soldier or member of the Royal Air Force has not been killed on active service. As the press and media have made international events more immediate to us, we have registered the cost of continuing conflict. The desire to pay tribute, to remember, and to pray for peace, has not diminished.

Events in New York (9/11) and the London bombings (7/7) have further made us sense the fragility of the peace that we enjoy from day to day. Even in stable democracies, we can be caught up in tragedy that arises from misguided human passion. The violent loss of human life sometimes feels all too close, and we can feel very near to those who died and to those who now grieve. We wish, somehow, to express our solidarity with them; to hold them in mind.

Remembering can be a private matter, but sometimes it seems fitting that it should be something shared and public. While always personal, it can be corporate and binding. This book, *They Shall Grow Not Old*, is a valuable resource for us as we come together on occasions to remember those who have died in war and acts of violence and terror. I commend it to all who will lead Ceremonies of Remembrance in these fragile times, and to all who believe that remembering the past has its place in the building of a better future.

✠David Conner
Bishop to Her Majesty's Forces

INTRODUCTION

The liturgical developments of the twentieth century brought with them an ever increasing attention to structural clarity in worship. The new services became easier to understand not only because of the use of contemporary language, but because they were designed with a clear and disciplined structure; and because great attention was given to the development of new typographical conventions – how the words were laid on the page.

Patterns for Worship (1995) and its successor *New Patterns for Worship* (2002) took another step forward in presenting a modular approach to the design of church services. The essential elements of a service were thematically presented to enable a minister to craft a service for many different occasions in any of the seasons. This book adopts that modular approach to the design of an act of worship for Remembrancetide, or for a service to focus on the vocation of the Armed Forces or their veterans' associations.

In this book you will find printed in full the texts authorized or commended for use by the competent liturgical authorities of the United Kingdom; you will find sample services to suit a number of different styles and circumstances; and you will find a range of material conveniently presented as basic building blocks from which you may assemble your own services. On the CD you will find the whole text to make it easy to craft your own Services of Remembrance; and you will find some ready-to-print standard forms.

SOURCES AND ACKNOWLEDGEMENTS

The services in this book contain material taken from *The Book of Common Prayer*, *Common Worship: Services and Prayers for the Church of England*, *The Book of Common Order of the Church of Scotland* together with material that I have written myself. Full details are listed below.

Scripture quotations are from the New Revised Standard Version of the Bible, Anglicized Edition, copyright 1989, 1995 by the Division of Christian Education of the National Council of the Churches of Christ in the USA. Used by permission. All rights reserved.

The Book of Common Order, St Andrew Press, 1994, copyright © The Office for Worship and Doctrine, Mission and Discipleship Council of the Church of Scotland. Used by permission.

Common Worship: Services and Prayers for the Church of England, Church House Publishing, 2000.

Common Worship: Daily Prayer, Preliminary Edition, Church House Publishing, 2002.

Common Worship: Daily Prayer, Church House Publishing, 2005.

Common Worship: Pastoral Services, Church House Publishing, 2000, second edition, 2004.

Common Worship texts are copyright © The Archbishops' Council and are reproduced by permission.

New Patterns for Worship, Church House Publishing, 2002.

The Promise of His Glory, Church House Publishing, 1984, 1990.

The Lord's Prayer from *Common Worship* is the English Language Liturgical Consultation translation from *Praying Together* © ELLC, 1988.

The Apostles' Creed and Lord's Prayer from *The Book of Common Prayer*, the rights in which are vested in the Crown, reproduced by permission of the Crown's Patentee, Cambridge University Press.

ABBREVIATIONS

BCO	*The Book of Common Order of the Church of Scotland*
BE	Brian Elliott CF
CW	*Common Worship: Services and Prayers for the Church of England*
CWDP	*Common Worship: Daily Prayer*
CWDPP	*Common Worship: Daily Prayer*, Preliminary Edition
CWPS	*Common Worship: Pastoral Services*
NP	*New Patterns for Worship*
SR 1968	The Service of Remembrance 1968 (from *The Promise of His Glory*)
SR 2005	The Service of Remembrance 2005 (Churches Together in Britain and Ireland)

PATTERNS

FOR

REMEMBRANCE

PATTERNS FOR REMEMBRANCE

The building bricks with which to create a service are outlined below. The Act of Remembrance and the Silence are clearly the essential components, and some conclusion to this act is necessary. This could be the Kohima Epitaph, or a prayer of Commemoration, or both. Everything else is optional, and ministers must use their own judgement to gauge the fullness of the rite. Tactful choices may need to be made when Christians are joined by members of other faith communities.

A bidding is good to set the terms of reference, but not essential. An Act of Commitment honours the view that remembering the past should focus our determination to build a better future, but the ceremony could end without. Time and circumstance should determine whether the Holy Scriptures should be read and expounded at some length, or presented in crisp sentences. The amount of praise or intercessory prayer, and its style, is another matter for the judgement of the minister.

The national official orders offer plenty of material with slightly different presentations, the sample services offer other possible solutions, and the material on the CD makes more suggestions. Look at the basic bricks, review the sample solutions, then craft your own service for those who will assemble on the day.

Greeting

A formal liturgical greeting – on many occasions it should not be used.

Bidding

A short paragraph to set the scene.

Sentence

Sentences of Scripture which may be used for focus, or be recited in order to start the silence exactly at 11 o'clock.

Penitence

Confessions, Kyries and other penitential texts.

Opening Prayer
> A theme prayer to start the service or introduce the liturgy of the word.

Remembrance
> The formal Act of Remembrance including the silence.

Commemoration
> The conclusion of the Act of Remembrance with a prayer.

Reading
> Scriptural readings.

Prayer
> Prayers of intercession which may end with the Lord's Prayer.

Litany
> Another form of intercession.

Responsory
> A third form of intercessory prayer.

Commitment
> An act of dedication for the future.

Kohima Epitaph
> Poignant words to bring the service or the Act of Remembrance to a conclusion.

Ending
> A blessing or other ending.

*Items below marked * are most suitable when other faith communities attend these Christian rites. Words in parenthesis may be omitted.*

GREETING

1

Grace, mercy and peace from God our Father
and the Lord Jesus Christ be with you

All **and also with you.**

2*

Blessed are the peacemakers:
they shall be called children of God.
(We meet in the name of Christ and share his peace.)

The peace of the Lord be always with you

All **and also with you.**

3

Jesus says to his disciples,
'Peace I leave with you; my peace I give you.
Not as the world gives do I give to you.
Let not your hearts be troubled or afraid.'

The peace of the Lord be always with you

All **and also with you.**

4

Peace to you from God who is our Father.
Peace from Jesus Christ who is our peace.
Peace from the Holy Spirit who gives us life.

The peace of the Lord be always with you

All **and also with you.**

5

Jesus says: 'Peace I leave with you; my peace I give to you.
Do not let your hearts be troubled, neither let them be afraid.'

The peace of the Lord be always with you

All **and also with you.**

BIDDING

1*

We worship God,
who is good and just and true.
He created and sustains the world;
and loves us, though we have failed him.
We remember
all who have given their lives in the struggle for justice and peace,
all who suffer in war and conflict,
and all who live in terror.
We ask for God's guidance and blessing,
that we may do his will,
and that all peoples may acknowledge his kingship and reign.

SR 1968, adapted

2*

We remember with thanksgiving and sorrow those whose lives,
in world wars and conflicts past and present,
have been given and taken away.

We pray for all who in bereavement, disability and pain
continue to suffer the consequences of fighting and terror.

We commit ourselves to work in penitence and faith
for reconciliation between the nations,
that all people may live together in freedom, justice and peace.

SR 2005, adapted; see page 128 for original

3*

Let us offer our thanksgivings to Almighty God,
for the victory achieved on land, at sea, and in the air,
and for the liberation of so many
from the cruelty of occupation and oppression.
Let us give thanks for the heroism and courage of those
who served in the armed services;
who worked on the home front in civil defence,
hospitals and relief agencies;
in factories, shops and farms.
And let us pray for those who endured captivity, torture, or death
that others might be free.

World War II Sixtieth Anniversary Service, adapted

4*

We are met this day
to glorify God who sustains the world;
To remember with thanksgiving
those who lived and died
in the service of our country;
and to ask for God's help and blessing
that we may be worthy of their sacrifice
each day of our life.

BCO

5*

We have come here today
to worship God our maker and sustainer,
to ask his forgiveness for all we do to spoil and destroy,
to remember those who have died working for peace,
and to pray for those who suffer the terror of war.

BE

6

We have come together in the name of Christ
to offer our praise and thanksgiving,
to hear and receive God's holy word,
to pray for the needs of the world,
(to remember those who have suffered in conflict, war and terror,)
and to seek the forgiveness of our sins,
that by the power of the Holy Spirit
we may give ourselves to the service of God.

CW, adapted

SENTENCE

OLD TESTAMENT SENTENCES

God is our refuge and strength;
a very present help in trouble.

Psalm 46.1

Whoever dwells in the shelter of the Most High
and abides under the shadow of the Almighty,
Shall say to the Lord, 'My refuge and my stronghold,
my God, in whom I put my trust.'

Psalm 91.1–2

I lift up my eyes to the hills;
from where is my help to come?
My help comes from the Lord,
the maker of heaven and earth.

Psalm 121.1–2

This I call to mind,
and therefore I have hope:
the steadfast love of the Lord never ceases,
his mercies never come to an end;
they are new every morning.

Lamentations 3.21–23

Those who wait for the Lord shall renew their strength,
they shall mount up with wings like eagles,
they shall run and not be weary,
they shall walk and not faint.

Isaiah 40.31

What does the Lord require of you
but to do justice, and to love kindness,
and to walk humbly with your God?

Micah 6.8

NEW TESTAMENT SENTENCES

Blessed are the peacemakers,
for they will be called children of God.

Matthew 5.9

Peace I leave with you; my peace I give to you.
I do not give to you as the world gives.
Do not let your hearts be troubled,
and do not let them be afraid.

John 14.27

No one has greater love than this,
to lay down one's life for one's friends.

John 15.13

Jesus said, 'In the world you face persecution.
But take courage; I have conquered the world.'

John 16.33

The wisdom from above is first pure,
then peaceable, gentle, willing to yield,
full of mercy and good fruits,
without a trace of partiality or hypocrisy.
And a harvest of righteousness is sown in peace
for those who make peace.

James 3.17–18

This is the message we have heard from him and proclaim to you,
that God is light and in him there is no darkness at all.

1 John 1.5

Blessed be the God and Father of our Lord Jesus Christ,
the Father of mercies and God of all consolation,
who consoles us in all our affliction,
so that we may be able to console those who are in any affliction,
with the consolation with which we ourselves are consoled by God.

2 Corinthians 1.3–4

SENTENCES OF REMEMBRANCE
Another set which all contain the word 'Remember'.

All the ends of the earth shall remember
and turn to the Lord;
and all the families of the nations
shall bow before him.

Psalm 22.27

Remember how short my time is –
how frail you have made all mortal flesh.

Psalms 89.47

The righteous will never be shaken;
they will be held in everlasting remembrance.

Psalm 112.6

Do not rejoice over anyone's death;
remember that we must all die.

Ecclesiasticus 8.7

Remember the commandments,
and do not be angry with your neighbour;
remember the covenant of the Most High,
and overlook faults.

Ecclesiasticus 28.7

Then I remembered your mercy, O Lord,
and your kindness from of old,
for you rescue those who wait for you
and save them from the hand of their enemies.

Ecclesiasticus 51.8

Jesus, remember me when you come into your kingdom.

Luke 23.42

Remember how Jesus told you, while he was still in Galilee,
that the Son of Man must be handed over to sinners,
and be crucified, and on the third day rise again.

Luke 24.6–7

*These sentences, or a psalm such as Psalm 91, may be recited in order to start the
silence exactly at 11 o'clock.*

PENITENCE

1

The minister says

>Let us confess to God
>the sins and shortcomings of the world;
>its pride, its selfishness, its greed;
>its evil divisions and hatreds.
>Let us confess our share in what is wrong,
>and our failure to seek and establish that peace
>which God wills for his children.

After a short silence, all say

All   **Most merciful God,**
we confess that we have sinned
in thought, word, and deed.
We have not loved you with our whole heart.
We have not loved our neighbours as ourselves.
In your mercy
forgive what we have been,
help us to amend what we are,
and direct what we shall be;
that we may do justly, love mercy,
and walk humbly with you;
through Jesus Christ our Lord.
Amen.

The minister stands and says

>Almighty God, have mercy upon us,
>pardon and deliver us from all our sins,
>confirm and strengthen us in all goodness,
>and keep us in life eternal;
>through Jesus Christ our Lord.

All   **Amen.**

SR 1968

2

Gathered together as God's family,
let us ask forgiveness from our heavenly Father,
for he is full of gentleness and compassion.

All **Lord God,**
we have sinned against you;
we have done evil in your sight.
We are sorry and repent.
Have mercy on us according to your love.
Wash away our wrongdoing
and cleanse us from our sin.
Renew a right spirit within us
and restore us to the joy of your salvation;
through Jesus Christ our Lord.
Amen.

The presiding minister says this or some other absolution
May the Father of all mercies cleanse *you* from *your* sins,
and restore *you* in his image to the praise and glory of his name,
through Jesus Christ our Lord.

All **Amen.**

3

Lord God our Father, maker of all:
we praise you for your great work creating the world.
Give us the skill to build a society where all may thrive,
and forgive us when we use your gifts poorly.
Lord, have mercy.

All **Lord, have mercy.**

Lord Jesus Christ,
Son of the living God,
Prince of Peace:
as we thank you for your life among us,
forgive us when we fail to live together as one family.
Help us to dwell together in love and peace,
seeking one another's welfare,
bearing one another's burdens,
and sharing one another's joys.
Christ, have mercy.

All **Christ, have mercy.**

Holy Spirit,
Lord of grace,
fulfiller of humanity:
give us strength to face the future,
and wisdom to learn from the past
as we remember those who have given their lives
in the service of justice and peace.
Lord, have mercy.

All **Lord, have mercy.**

BE

The presiding minister may say this or another absolution
The almighty and merciful Lord
grant *you* pardon and forgiveness of all *your* sins,
time for amendment of life,
and the grace and strength of the Holy Spirit.

All **Amen.**

CW

These words may follow any rite of penance
Holy God, holy and mighty, holy and immortal:
have mercy upon us.

All **Holy God, holy and mighty, holy and immortal:
have mercy upon us.**

OPENING PRAYER

1*

Father of all mercies:
grant that our remembrance this day
may be consecrated for practical service
and the world made better
for our children's children.

All   (**Amen.**)

BCO, adapted

2*

Stir up your power, O God,
and come among us.
Heal our wounds,
calm our fears
and give us peace;
(through Jesus our Redeemer.

All   **Amen.**)

CW, Advent

3*

Lord our God,
our sure stronghold,
hear the voice of our pleading
and deliver us from every evil.
Strengthen us as we strive for the poor and oppressed,
and establish your justice in all the earth.

All   (**Amen.**)

CWDPP, Psalm 140

4
    God of righteousness,
    you have taught us through your Son
    to set our minds on your kingdom and justice before all things.
    Grant that in us and in others
    suspicion may give place to trust,
    and stridency to peace,
    that we may live and work together in unity and love;
    through Jesus Christ our Lord.

All **Amen.**

BCO

REMEMBRANCE

1

The minister or another says
    Let us remember before God,
    and commend to his sure keeping:
    those who have died for their country in conflict;
    those whom we knew, and whose memory we treasure;
    and all who have lived and died in the service of humanity.

A second (older) voice may continue
    They shall grow not old as we that are left grow old:
    Age shall not weary them, nor the years condemn.

A third (younger) voice may conclude
    At the going down of the sun and in the morning
    We will remember them.

All **We will remember them.**

SR 1968, adapted

    (The Last Post)   *(The Lament)*   *The Silence*   *(The Reveille)*

*Wreath laying and other ceremonies may take place here, or after the
Commemoration.*

COMMEMORATION

1

Almighty and eternal God,
from whose love in Christ we cannot be parted,
either by death or life:
Hear our prayers and thanksgivings
for all whom we remember this day;
fulfil in them the purpose of your love;
and bring us all, with them, to your eternal joy;
through Jesus Christ our Lord.

All **Amen.**

SR 1968

2

Most merciful God,
we remember those whom you have gathered
from the storm of war into the peace of your presence:
grant that we, being faithful till death,
may receive with them the crown of life that never fades,
through Jesus Christ our Lord.

All **Amen.**

BE

3

Ever-living God,
we remember those whom you have gathered
from the storm of war into the peace of your presence;
may that same peace calm our fears,
bring justice to all peoples
and establish harmony among the nations,
through Jesus Christ our Lord.

All **Amen.**

SR 2005 (BE)

4*

Remember, Lord, your people, who cry to you in their grief.
Remember the fallen in battle, and the innocents who have died.
Remember your power to heal and save.

BE

READING

Readings may be chosen from the collection below, or the minister may make other provision.

In days to come
the mountain of the Lord's house
shall be established as the highest of the mountains,
and shall be raised above the hills;
all the nations shall stream to it.
Many peoples shall come and say,
'Come, let us go up to the mountain of the Lord,
to the house of the God of Jacob;
that he may teach us his ways
and that we may walk in his paths.'
For out of Zion shall go forth instruction,
and the word of the Lord from Jerusalem.
He shall judge between the nations,
and shall arbitrate for many peoples;
they shall beat their swords into ploughshares,
and their spears into pruning-hooks;
nation shall not lift up sword against nation,
neither shall they learn war any more.

O house of Jacob,
come, let us walk
in the light of the Lord!

Isaiah 2.2—5

In days to come
the mountain of the Lord's house
shall be established as the highest of the mountains,
and shall be raised up above the hills.
Peoples shall stream to it,
and many nations shall come and say:
'Come, let us go up to the mountain of the Lord,
to the house of the God of Jacob;
that he may teach us his ways
and that we may walk in his paths.'
For out of Zion shall go forth instruction,
and the word of the Lord from Jerusalem.
He shall judge between many peoples,
and shall arbitrate between strong nations far away;
they shall beat their swords into ploughshares,
and their spears into pruning-hooks;
nation shall not lift up sword against nation,
neither shall they learn war any more;
but they shall all sit under their own vines
     and under their own fig trees,
and no one shall make them afraid;
for the mouth of the Lord of hosts has spoken.

For all the peoples walk,
each in the name of its god,
but we will walk in the name of the Lord our God
for ever and ever.

Micah 4.1—5

But the souls of the righteous are in the hand of God,
and no torment will ever touch them.
In the eyes of the foolish they seemed to have died,
and their departure was thought to be a disaster,
and their going from us to be their destruction;
but they are at peace.
For though in the sight of others they were punished,
their hope is full of immortality.

Having been disciplined a little, they will receive great good,
because God tested them and found them worthy of himself;
like gold in the furnace he tried them,
and like a sacrificial burnt-offering he accepted them.
In the time of their visitation they will shine forth,
and will run like sparks through the stubble.
They will govern nations and rule over peoples,
and the Lord will reign over them for ever.

Wisdom 3.1–8

When Jesus saw the crowds, he went up the mountain; and after he
sat down, his disciples came to him. Then he began to speak, and
taught them, saying:
    'Blessed are the poor in spirit,
        for theirs is the kingdom of heaven.
    Blessed are those who mourn,
        for they will be comforted.
    Blessed are the meek,
        for they will inherit the earth.
    Blessed are those who hunger and thirst for righteousness,
        for they will be filled.
    Blessed are the merciful,
        for they will receive mercy.
    Blessed are the pure in heart,
        for they will see God.
    Blessed are the peacemakers,
        for they will be called children of God.
    Blessed are those who are persecuted for righteousness' sake,
        for theirs is the kingdom of heaven.
'Blessed are you when people revile you and persecute you and utter
all kinds of evil against you falsely on my account. Rejoice and be
glad, for your reward is great in heaven, for in the same way they
persecuted the prophets who were before you.'

Matthew 5.1–12

Jesus said, 'As the Father has loved me, so I have loved you; abide in my love. If you keep my commandments, you will abide in my love, just as I have kept my Father's commandments and abide in his love. I have said these things to you so that my joy may be in you, and that your joy may be complete.

'This is my commandment, that you love one another as I have loved you. No one has greater love than this, to lay down one's life for one's friends. You are my friends if you do what I command you. I do not call you servants any longer, because the servant does not know what the master is doing; but I have called you friends, because I have made known to you everything that I have heard from my Father. You did not choose me but I chose you. And I appointed you to go and bear fruit, fruit that will last, so that the Father will give you whatever you ask him in my name. I am giving you these commands so that you may love one another.'

John 15.9–17

Be strong in the Lord and in the strength of his power. Put on the whole armour of God, so that you may be able to stand against the wiles of the devil. For our struggle is not against enemies of blood and flesh, but against the rulers, against the authorities, against the cosmic powers of this present darkness, against the spiritual forces of evil in the heavenly places. Therefore take up the whole armour of God, so that you may be able to withstand on that evil day, and having done everything, to stand firm. Stand therefore, and fasten the belt of truth around your waist, and put on the breastplate of righteousness. As shoes for your feet put on whatever will make you ready to proclaim the gospel of peace. With all of these, take the shield of faith, with which you will be able to quench all the flaming arrows of the evil one. Take the helmet of salvation, and the sword of the Spirit, which is the word of God.

Ephesians 6.10–17

PRAYER

INTRODUCTION TO PRAYER

> In the power of the Spirit,
> and in union with Christ,
> let us pray to the Father.

SHORT PRAYERS

1 *For the departed*

> Lord,
> welcome into your calm and peaceful kingdom
> those who have departed out of this present life to be with you.
> Grant them rest and a place with the spirits of the just;
> and give them the life that knows no age,
> the reward that passes not away.

All **Amen.**

Ignatius of Loyola (1491–1556)

2 *For those who suffer*

> God of our joys and sorrows,
> comfort the exiled, console the oppressed
> and bring us in joy to our true home,
> where your faithful servants sing your praise.

All **Amen.**

CWDPP, Psalm 137

3 *For the leaders of the nations*

> Go before us, O Lord,
> with the blessings of your goodness
> and guide all those you call to authority
> in the way of your justice,
> the knowledge of your liberty
> and the wisdom of your gentleness.

All **Amen.**

CWDPP, Psalm 21

4 For faith

How generous is your goodness, O God,
how great is your salvation,
how faithful is your love.
Help us to trust in you in trial,
to praise you in deliverance
and to rejoice before you with overflowing hearts.

All **Amen.**

CWDPP, Psalm 66

5 For peace

God of our joy and gladness,
hear our prayer for the peace of this world
and bring us at last,
with all our companions in faith,
to the peace of that city where you live and reign,
Father, Son and Holy Spirit,
now and to all eternity.

All **Amen.**

CWDPP, Psalm 122

6 For protection

O Father, your power is greater than all powers.
O Son, under your leadership we cannot fear anything.
O Spirit, under your protection
    there is nothing we cannot overcome.

A prayer of the Kikuyu, Kenya

7 For the rule of God to be established

Your kingdom come, O Lord,
with deliverance for the needy,
with peace for the righteous,
with overflowing blessing for all nations,
with glory, honour and praise
for the only Saviour,
Jesus Christ our Lord.

All **Amen.**

CWDPP, Psalm 72

FORMAL PRAYERS

1 For the peace of the world

> Almighty God,
> from whom all thoughts of truth and peace proceed:
> kindle, we pray, in the hearts of all, the true love of peace
> and guide with your pure and peaceable wisdom
> those who take counsel for the nations of the earth
> that in tranquillity your kingdom may go forward,
> till the earth is filled with the knowledge of your love;
> through Jesus Christ your Son our Lord.

All **Amen.**

CW

2 In time of war

> God of infinite mercy,
> we trust in your good purposes of peace for all your children.
> We pray for those who at this time
> > face danger in the defence of justice.
> Watch over those in peril;
> support those who are anxious for loved ones;
> gather into your eternal purpose those who will die.
> Remove from the hearts of all people
> the passions that keep alive the spirit of war,
> and in your goodness restore peace among us;
> for the sake of the Prince of peace,
> Jesus Christ our Lord.

All **Amen.**

BCO

3 For the Forces of the Crown

Almighty God, in you alone we find safety and peace.
We commend to your gracious keeping
all the men and women
who serve in the Navy, the Army, or the Air Force,
who face danger and put their lives at risk
so that others might live in safety.
Defend them day by day by your heavenly power;
and help them to know
that they can never pass beyond the reach of your care.
Keep alive in them and in us your vision of that peace
which alone we must seek and serve;
through Jesus Christ our Lord.

All **Amen.**

BCO

4 For the Armed Forces

Almighty God,
stretch forth your mighty arm
to strengthen and protect the armed forces:
grant that meeting danger with courage
and all occasions with discipline and loyalty,
they may truly serve the cause of justice and peace;
to the honour of your holy name,
through Jesus Christ our Lord.

All **Amen.**

5 For the victims of war

> God of love, whose compassion never fails;
> we bring before you
>> the griefs and perils of peoples and nations;
>> the necessities of the homeless;
>> the helplessness of the aged and weak;
>> the sighings of prisoners;
>> the pains of the sick and injured;
>> the sorrow of the bereaved.
> Comfort and relieve them, O merciful Father,
> according to their needs;
> for the sake of your Son,
> our Saviour Jesus Christ.

All **Amen.**

Anselm (1033–1109)

6 For social justice and responsibility

> Eternal God,
> in whose perfect realm
> no sword is drawn but the sword of righteousness,
> and no strength known but the strength of love:
> so guide and inspire the work of those who seek your kingdom
> that all your people may find their security
> in that love which casts out fear
> and in the fellowship revealed to us
> in Jesus Christ our Saviour.

All **Amen.**

CW

7 That the will of God may prevail

Lord God,
Sovereign over all,
bring in the day of the splendour of your kingdom
and draw the whole world into willing obedience to your reign.
Cast out the evil things that cause war,
and send your Spirit
to rule the hearts of people in righteousness and love.
Repair the desolations of many generations,
that the wilderness may rejoice,
and the city be made glad with your law.
Confirm every work that is founded on truth,
and fulfil the desires and hopes of your people,
through the victory of Christ our Lord.

All **Amen.**

BCO

8 For guidance and protection

God of light and love,
in your tender compassion
you sent your Son to shine on those who sit in darkness
and to guide our feet into the way of peace.
Grant us, in our doubts and uncertainties,
the grace to ask what you would have us do.
By your Spirit of wisdom, save us from false choices.
And since it is by your light that we are enlightened,
lead us and protect us,
and give us a straight path to follow,
that we may neither stumble nor fall;
through Jesus Christ our Lord.

All **Amen.**

BCO

9 For selfless commitment

> Teach us, good Lord,
> to serve you as you deserve;
> to give and not to count the cost;
> to fight and not to heed the wounds;
> to toil and not to seek for rest;
> to labour and not to seek for any reward,
> save that of knowing that we do your will.

All **Amen.**

Ignatius of Loyola (1491–1556)

10 Christaraksha: an Indian prayer for protection

*Depending on the context the word 'you' may be changed to 'us', 'him', 'her'
or 'them'.*

> May the cross of the Son of God,
> which is mightier than all the hosts of Satan
> and more glorious than all the hosts of heaven,
> abide with *you* in *your* going out and *your* coming in.
> By day and by night, at morning and at evening,
> at all times and in all places may it protect and defend *you*.
> From the wrath of evildoers, from the assaults of evil spirits,
> from foes visible and invisible, from the snares of the devil,
> from all passions that beguile the soul and body:
> may it guard, protect and deliver *you*.

All **Amen.**

CW, adapted

The Lord's Prayer may conclude the prayers and may be introduced with
these words

> Gathering our prayers and praises into one,
> let us pray with confidence
> as our Saviour has taught us.

All   **Our Father, who art in heaven,**
     hallowed be thy name;
     thy kingdom come;
     thy will be done;
     on earth as it is in heaven.
     Give us this day our daily bread.
     And forgive us our trespasses,
     as we forgive those who trespass against us.
     And lead us not into temptation;
     but deliver us from evil.
     For thine is the kingdom,
     the power, and the glory,
     for ever and ever.
     Amen.

Or else this version from Common Worship

> Gathering our prayers and praises into one,
> as our Saviour taught us, so we pray

All   **Our Father in heaven,**
     hallowed be your name,
     your kingdom come,
     your will be done,
     on earth as in heaven.
     Give us today our daily bread.
     Forgive us our sins
     as we forgive those who sin against us.
     Lead us not into temptation
     but deliver us from evil.
     For the kingdom, the power,
     and the glory are yours
     now and for ever.
     Amen.

LITANY

A LITANY FOR THE ARMED FORCES

Holy God, the protector of all who trust in you:

Grant to the Armed Forces of the Crown,
and all who seek you,
the assurance of your presence,
the knowledge of your love,
and the guidance of your spirit.
Lord, hear us.

All **Lord, graciously hear us.**

Bring healing and wholeness to people and nations:
let your mercy rule all that we do.
Lord, hear us.

All **Lord, graciously hear us.**

Be with all who defend your truth and your peace,
that we may vanquish injustice and wrong.
Lord, hear us.

All **Lord, graciously hear us.**

Give wisdom to leaders and commanders,
that they may be a force for good on the Earth.
Lord, hear us.

All **Lord, graciously hear us.**

In your wisdom embrace our enemies,
and those who wish us harm:
turn the hearts of all to kindness and friendship.
Lord, hear us.

All **Lord, graciously hear us.**

Be with all medics and chaplains,
and all who support the suffering:
give them wisdom and skill, sympathy and patience.
Lord, hear us.

All **Lord, graciously hear us.**

Sustain the anxious and fearful,
and renew them with courage from on high.
Lord, hear us.

All **Lord, graciously hear us.**

Comfort all worried families, whose loved ones are in danger:
surround them with your love, protect them from all harm.
Lord, hear us.

All **Lord, graciously hear us.**

Be with the sick and wounded,
stand by all prisoners and captives:
let your mercy be shown to all, and your power to heal and save.
Lord, hear us.

All **Lord, graciously hear us.**

Receive those fallen in battle, and all innocents who have died:
surround their loved ones with compassion,
and give them a patient faith.
Lord, hear us.

All **Lord, graciously hear us.**

Confirm what is founded on truth,
and establish your love in our hearts;
that justice may abound on the Earth,
and all peoples rejoice in your peace.
Lord, hear us.

All **Lord, graciously hear us.**

BE

The litany may end with the Lord's Prayer, or else this or some other collect
Lord our God,
our sure stronghold,
hear the voice of our pleading
and deliver us from every evil.
Strengthen us as we strive for the poor and oppressed,
and establish your justice in all the earth.

All **Amen.**

CWDPP, Psalm 140

In peace let us pray to the Lord.

For the leaders of the nations,
that you will guide them in the ways of freedom, justice and truth.
Lord, in your mercy

All **hear our prayer.**

For those who serve in the armed forces of the Crown,
that they may have discipline and discernment,
courage and compassion.
Lord, in your mercy

All **hear our prayer.**

For our enemies, and those who wish us harm,
that you may turn the hearts of all to kindness and friendship.
Lord, in your mercy

All **hear our prayer.**

For the wounded and the captive, the grieving and the homeless,
that in all their trials they may know your love and support.
Lord, in your mercy

All **hear our prayer.**

Most Holy God and Father,
hear our prayers for all who strive for peace,
and all who yearn for justice.
Help us, who today remember the cost of war,
to work for a better tomorrow;
and, as we commend to you lives lost in terror and conflict,
bring us all, in the end,
to the peace of your presence;
through Christ our Lord.

All **Amen.**

BE

Let us pray with hope for the future of the world
and for the needs of all people.

For peace and justice in our world,
for an end to war and conflict,
for the leaders of all nations and peoples,
and for those who make peace and foster reconciliation.
Lord, in your mercy

All   **hear our prayer.**

For the unity of all Christian people,
for the Church of God in every land,
for all who seek God and the truth,
and for all who follow the way of conscience with integrity.
Lord, in your mercy

All   **hear our prayer.**

For the healing of memories,
for those who suffer as a result of war,
for communities where past wrongs and violence persist,
for all in pain or distress and those who care for them.
Lord, in your mercy

All   **hear our prayer.**

For friendship and trust amongst all,
for an appreciation of our interdependence,
for the new partnerships between the nations,
and for a world that is in harmony with itself.
Lord, in your mercy

All   **hear our prayer.**

Most merciful Father,
accept our prayers
that we may know your peace in our hearts,
and your love in our lives,
through Christ our Lord.

All   **Amen.**

World War II Sixtieth Anniversary Service, adapted

A LITANY FOR TROOPS IN DANGER

In peace let us pray to the Lord.

For the people of God,
that they may worship you in spirit and in truth,
let us pray to the Lord:

All **Lord, have mercy.**

For the leaders of the nations,
that you will guide them in the ways of justice, mercy and truth,
let us pray to the Lord:

All **Lord, have mercy.**

For the peacemakers, that you may protect them from all evil,
let us pray to the Lord:

All **Lord, have mercy.**

For our loved ones, wherever they may be
and for those who wear the Queen's uniform on our behalf,
let us pray to the Lord:

All **Lord, have mercy.**

For our enemies, and those who wish us harm,
that you may turn the hearts of all to kindness and friendship,
let us pray to the Lord:

All **Lord, have mercy.**

For the sick and wounded,
and for all prisoners and captives,
that they may know your power to heal and save,
let us pray to the Lord:

All **Lord, have mercy.**

Almighty God,
you see that we have no power of ourselves to help ourselves:
keep us both outwardly in our bodies,
and inwardly in our souls;
that we may be defended from all adversities
     which may happen to the body,
and from all evil thoughts which may assault and hurt the soul;
through Jesus Christ our Lord.

All **Amen.**

But if there have been fatalities the above prayer may be omitted, and the litany continued into an Act of Remembrance

> For those who mourn …
> let us pray to the Lord:

All **Lord, have mercy.**

> For those who have died in the conflict …
> let us pray to the Lord:

All **Lord, have mercy.**

BE

> They shall grow not old as we that are left grow old:
> Age shall not weary them, nor the years condemn.
> At the going down of the sun and in the morning
> We will remember them.

All **We will remember them.**

> *(The Last Post)*   *The Silence*   *(The Reveille)*

> Most merciful and ever-living God,
> we remember those whom you have gathered
> from the storm of war into the peace of your presence:
> grant that we, being faithful till death,
> may receive with them the crown of life that never fades,
> through Jesus Christ our Lord.

All **Amen.**

RESPONSORY

1

Make your ways known upon earth, Lord God,

All **your saving power among all peoples.**

Renew your Church in holiness

All **and help us serve you with joy.**

Guide the leaders of this and every nation,

All **that justice may prevail throughout the world.**

Let not the needy be forgotten,

All **nor the hope of the poor be taken away.**

Make us instruments of your peace

All **and let your glory be over all the earth.**

NP

2

Send forth your strength, O God,

All **establish what you have wrought in us.**

Uphold all those who fall

All **and raise up those who are bowed down.**

Open the eyes of the blind

All **and set the prisoners free.**

Sustain the orphan and widow

All **and give food to those who hunger.**

Grant them the joy of your help again

All **and sustain them with your Spirit.**

O Lord, judge the peoples

All **and take all nations for your own.**

CWDP

3

O Lord, answer us in the day of trouble,
All **send us help from your holy place.**

Show us the path of life,
All **for in your presence is joy.**

Give justice to the orphan and oppressed
All **and break the power of wickedness and evil.**

Look upon the hungry and sorrowful
All **and grant them the help for which they long.**

Let the heavens rejoice and the earth be glad;
All **may your glory endure for ever.**

Your kingship has dominion over all
All **and with you is our redemption.**

CWDP

4

Save your people, Lord, and bless your inheritance.
All **Govern and uphold them now and always.**

Day by day, we bless you.
All **We praise your name for ever.**

Keep us today, Lord, from all sin.
All **Have mercy on us, Lord, have mercy.**

We long for your salvation, O Lord:
All **grant us understanding, that we may live.**

Lord, show us your love and mercy,
All **for we put our trust in you.**

In you, Lord, is our hope:
All **let us not be confounded at the last.**

CWDP

COMMITMENT

1*

Let us pledge ourselves anew
to the service of God and humanity:
that we may help, encourage, and comfort others,
and support those working for the relief of the needy
and for the peace and welfare of the nations.

All **Lord God our Father,**
we pledge ourselves
to serve you and all your peoples,
in the cause of peace,
for the relief of want and suffering,
and for the praise of your name.
Guide us by your Spirit;
give us wisdom;
give us courage;
give us hope;
and keep us faithful
now and always.
Amen.

SR 1968, adapted

2*

Let us commit ourselves to responsible living and faithful service.

Will you strive for all that makes for peace?

All   **We will.**

Will you seek to heal the wounds of war?

All   **We will.**

Will you work for a just future for all humanity?

All   **We will.**

Merciful God,
we offer to you the fears in us
that have not yet been cast out by love:
May we accept the hope you have placed
in the hearts of all people,
And live lives of justice, courage and mercy;
(through Jesus Christ our risen Redeemer.)

All   **(Amen.)**

SR 2005

Or the minister may say the 1968 Prayer of Commitment above.

3*

A reader says

> Will you honour all who bore the pains and adversities of war?
> Will you offer them your help and support,
> and protect their dignity and welfare?

All **With the help of God, we will.**

> Will you remember the causes for which they endured adversity
> and for which many fought and died,
> by promoting peace, justice and harmony among all people?

All **With the help of God, we will.**

> Will you always acknowledge how precious are the gifts
> which God has entrusted to us,
> and exercise the freedoms and opportunities you have
> with gratitude and humility?

All **With the help of God, we will.**

The presiding minister says

> May Almighty God,
> who has given us the will to undertake these things,
> give us also the strength to perform them:
> for his name's sake.

All **Amen.**

World War II Sixtieth Anniversary Service

KOHIMA EPITAPH

> When you go home tell them of us and say:
> 'For your tomorrow, we gave our today.'

ENDING

1*

> May the Lord bless us and watch over us,
> may the Lord make his face shine upon us and be gracious to us,
> may the Lord look kindly on us and give us peace.

Numbers 6.24–26

2

> May God grant to the living, grace;
> to the departed, rest;
> to the Church, the Queen, the Commonwealth, and all people,
>   peace and concord;
> and to us and all his servants, life everlasting;
> and the blessing of God almighty,
> Father, Son, and Holy Spirit,
> come down upon you and remain with you always.

All **Amen.**

SR 1968, adapted

3

> May God give *you* his comfort and his peace,
> his light and his joy,
> in this world and the next;
> and the blessing of God almighty,
> the Father, the Son, and the Holy Spirit,
> be among you and remain with you always.

All **Amen.**

CWPS, Funeral

4

Go forth into the world in peace;
be of good courage;
hold fast that which is good;
render to no one evil for evil;
strengthen the faint-hearted;
support the weak;
help the afflicted;
honour everyone;
love and serve the Lord,
rejoicing in the power of the Holy Spirit;
and the blessing of God almighty,
the Father, the Son, and the Holy Spirit,
be among you and remain with you always.

All **Amen.**

5

May the God of all power and might
make you strong in faith and love,
defend you on every side,
and guide you in truth and peace;
and the blessing of God almighty,
the Father, the Son, and the Holy Spirit,
be among you and remain with you always.

All **Amen.**

6

The love of the Lord Jesus draw *you* to himself,
the power of the Lord Jesus strengthen *you* in his service,
the joy of the Lord Jesus fill *your* hearts;
and the blessing of God almighty,
the Father, the Son, and the Holy Spirit,
be among you and remain with you always.

All **Amen.**

SAMPLE
SERVICES

1 A SIMPLE CEREMONY OF REMEMBRANCE

At a war memorial when Christians are joined by other faith communities.
Minimal congregational response is required.

SENTENCE

God is our refuge and strength,
a very present help in trouble.

Psalm 46.1

OPENING PRAYER

The presiding minister says
Stir up your power, O God,
and come among us.
Heal our wounds,
calm our fears
and give us peace.

CW

REMEMBRANCE

The presiding minister says
Let us remember before God,
and commend to his sure keeping:
those who have died for their country in conflict;
those whom we knew, and whose memory we treasure;
and all who have lived and died in the service of humanity.

A second (older) voice says
They shall grow not old as we that are left grow old:
Age shall not weary them, nor the years condemn.

A third (younger) voice says
At the going down of the sun and in the morning
We will remember them.

All **We will remember them.**

SR 1968, adapted

(The Last Post)   The Silence   (The Reveille)

> When you go home tell them of us and say:
> 'For your tomorrow, we gave our today.'

Wreath laying and other ceremonies may take place here, or after the commemoration.

COMMEMORATION

The presiding minister says

> Remember, Lord, your people, who cry to you in their grief.
> Remember the fallen in battle, and the innocents who have died.
> Remember your power to heal and save.

PRAYER

For the departed

> Lord,
> welcome into your calm and peaceful kingdom
> those who have departed out of this present life to be with you.
> Grant them rest and a place with the spirits of the just;
> and give them the life that knows no age,
> the reward that passes not away.

Ignatius of Loyola (1491–1556)

For those who suffer

> God of our joys and sorrows,
> comfort the exiled, console the oppressed
> and bring us in joy to our true home,
> where your faithful servants sing your praise.

CWDPP, Psalm 137

For the Queen and Parliament, and for the leaders of all the nations

> Go before us, O Lord,
> with the blessings of your goodness
> and guide all those you call to authority
> in the way of your justice,
> the knowledge of your liberty
> and the wisdom of your gentleness.

CWDPP, Psalm 21

For faith by which to live
How generous is your goodness, O God,
how great is your salvation,
how faithful is your love.
Help us to trust in you in trial,
to praise you in deliverance
and to rejoice before you with overflowing hearts.

CWDPP, Psalm 66

COMMITMENT

This prayer may be said by the minister or another single voice, or by the whole congregation.
Lord God our Father,
we pledge ourselves
to serve you and all your peoples,
in the cause of peace,
for the relief of want and suffering,
and for the praise of your name.
Guide us by your Spirit;
give us wisdom;
give us courage;
give us hope;
and keep us faithful
now and always.

All **Amen.**

SR 1968, adapted

ENDING

The presiding minister says
May the Lord bless us and watch over us,
may the Lord make his face shine upon us and be gracious to us,
may the Lord look kindly on us and give us peace.

Numbers 6.24–26

2 A CEREMONY OF REMEMBRANCE
at a war memorial

BIDDING

Let us offer our thanksgivings to Almighty God,
for the victory achieved on land, at sea, and in the air,
and for the liberation of so many
from the cruelty of occupation and oppression.
Let us give thanks for the heroism and courage of those
who served in the armed services;
who worked on the home front in civil defence,
hospitals and relief agencies;
in factories, shops and farms.
And let us pray for those who endured captivity, torture, or death
that others might be free.

REMEMBRANCE

The presiding minister says

Let us remember before God,
and commend to his sure keeping:
those who have died for their country in war;
those whom we knew, and whose memory we treasure;
and all who have lived and died in the service of humanity.

A second (older) voice says

They shall grow not old as we that are left grow old:
Age shall not weary them, nor the years condemn.

A third (younger) voice says

At the going down of the sun and in the morning
We will remember them.

All **We will remember them.**

SR 1968, adapted

(The Last Post)   *The Silence*   *(The Reveille)*

*Wreath laying and other ceremonies may take place here, or after the
commemoration.*

COMMEMORATION

The presiding minister says

Most merciful and ever-living God,
we remember those whom you have gathered
from the storm of war into the peace of your presence:
grant that we, being faithful till death,
may receive with them the crown of life that never fades,
through Jesus Christ our Lord.

All **Amen.**

HYMN

Eternal Father, strong to save,
Whose arm doth bind the restless wave,
Who bid'st the mighty ocean deep
Its own appointed limits keep;
O hear us when we cry to thee,
for those in peril on the sea.

O Christ, the Universal Lord,
who suffered death by nails and sword,
from all assault of deadly foe
sustain thy soldiers where they go;
and evermore hold in thy hand
all those in peril on the land.

O Holy Spirit, Lord of grace
Who fills with strength the human race;
Inspire us all to know the right,
Guide all who dare the eagle's flight;
And underneath thy wings of care
Guard all from peril in the air.

O Trinity of love and power!
Our brethren shield in danger's hour;
From rock and tempest, fire and foe,
Protect them wheresoe'er they go;
Thus evermore shall rise to thee,
Praise from the air, the land and sea.

verses 1,4: William Whiting (1825–78); verses 2,3: BE

READING

When Jesus saw the crowds, he went up the mountain; and after he
sat down, his disciples came to him. Then he began to speak, and
taught them, saying:
'Blessed are the poor in spirit,
for theirs is the kingdom of heaven.
Blessed are those who mourn,
for they will be comforted.
Blessed are the meek,
for they will inherit the earth.
Blessed are those who hunger and thirst for righteousness,
for they will be filled.
Blessed are the merciful,
for they will receive mercy.
Blessed are the pure in heart,
for they will see God.
Blessed are the peacemakers,
for they will be called children of God.
Blessed are those who are persecuted for righteousness' sake,
for theirs is the kingdom of heaven.
'Blessed are you when people revile you and persecute you and utter
all kinds of evil against you falsely on my account. Rejoice and be
glad, for your reward is great in heaven, for in the same way they
persecuted the prophets who were before you.'

Matthew 5. 1–12

PRAYER

For peace
God of our joy and gladness,
hear our prayer for the peace of this world
and bring us at last,
with all our companions in faith,
to the peace of that city where you live and reign,
Father, Son and Holy Spirit,
now and to all eternity.

All **Amen.**

CWDPP, Psalm 122

For protection

    O Father, your power is greater than all powers.

    O Son, under your leadership we cannot fear anything.

    O Spirit, under your protection

        there is nothing we cannot overcome.

A prayer of the Kikuyu, Kenya

For the rule of God to be established

    Your kingdom come, O Lord,

    with deliverance for the needy,

    with peace for the righteous,

    with overflowing blessing for all nations,

    with glory, honour and praise

    for the only Saviour,

    Jesus Christ our Lord.

All   **Amen.**

CWDPP, Psalm 72

COMMITMENT

    Let us pledge ourselves anew

    to the service of God and humanity:

    that we may help, encourage, and comfort others,

    and support those working for the relief of the needy

    and for the peace and welfare of the nations.

All   **Lord God our Father,**

    we pledge ourselves

    to serve you and all your peoples,

    in the cause of peace,

    for the relief of want and suffering,

    and for the praise of your name.

    Guide us by your Spirit;

    give us wisdom;

    give us courage;

    give us hope;

    and keep us faithful

    now and always.

    Amen.

SR 1968, adapted

All   **God save our gracious Queen,**
      Long live our noble Queen,
      God save the Queen.
      Send her victorious,
      Happy and glorious,
      Long to reign over us:
      God save the Queen.

ENDING

    May God grant to the living, grace;

    to the departed, rest;

    to the Church, the Queen, the Commonwealth, and all people,
        peace and concord;

    and to us and all his servants, life everlasting;

    and the blessing of God almighty,

    Father, Son, and Holy Spirit,

    come down upon you and remain with you always.

All   **Amen.**

SR 1968, adapted

3 A SERVICE FOR REMEMBRANCE SUNDAY
in Church

THE PREPARATION

Blessed are the peacemakers:
they shall be called children of God.
We meet in the name of Christ and share his peace.

The peace of the Lord be always with you
All **and also with you.**

PENITENCE

Lord God our Father, maker of all:
we praise you for your great work creating the world.
Give us the skill to build a society where all may thrive,
and forgive us when we use your gifts poorly.
Lord, have mercy.
All **Lord, have mercy.**

Lord Jesus Christ,
Son of the living God,
Prince of Peace:
as we thank you for your life among us,
forgive us when we fail to live together as one family.
Help us to dwell together in love and peace,
seeking one another's welfare,
bearing one another's burdens,
and sharing one another's joys.
Christ, have mercy.
All **Christ, have mercy.**

Holy Spirit, Lord of grace, fulfiller of humanity:
give us strength to face the future,
and wisdom to learn from the past
as we remember those who have given their lives
in the service of justice and peace.
Lord, have mercy.
All **Lord, have mercy.**

THE ACT OF REMEMBRANCE

REMEMBRANCE

The presiding minister says
>Let us remember before God,
>and commend to his sure keeping:
>those who have died for their country in conflict;
>those whom we knew, and whose memory we treasure;
>and all who have lived and died in the service of humanity.

A second voice may say
>They shall grow not old as we that are left grow old:
>Age shall not weary them, nor the years condemn.
>At the going down of the sun and in the morning
>We will remember them.

All   **We will remember them.**

SR 1968, adapted

(The Last Post)   *The Silence*   *(The Reveille)*

Wreath laying and other ceremonies may take place here, or after the commemoration.

COMMEMORATION

>Almighty and eternal God,
>from whose love in Christ we cannot be parted,
>either by death or life:
>Hear our prayers and thanksgivings
>for all whom we remember this day;
>fulfil in them the purpose of your love;
>and bring us all, with them, to your eternal joy;
>through Jesus Christ our Lord.

All   **Amen.**

SR 1968

> Rejoice, O land, in God thy might,
> his will obey, him serve aright;
> for thee the saints uplift their voice:
> fear not, O land, in God rejoice.
>
> Glad shalt thou be, with blessing crowned,
> with joy and peace thou shalt abound;
> yea, love with thee shall make his home
> until thou see God's kingdom come.
>
> He shall forgive thy sins untold:
> remember thou his love of old;
> walk in his way, his word adore,
> and keep his truth for evermore.

Robert Bridges (1844–1930)

THE SERVICE OF THE WORD

OPENING PRAYER

> Father of all mercies:
> grant that our remembrance this day
> may be consecrated for practical service
> and the world made better
> for our children's children.

BCO, adapted

FIRST READING

HYMN

SECOND READING

SERMON

HYMN

PRAYERS

In the power of the Spirit,
and in union with Christ,
let us pray to the Father.

Send forth your strength, O God,

All **establish what you have wrought in us.**

Uphold all those who fall

All **and raise up those who are bowed down.**

Open the eyes of the blind

All **and set the prisoners free.**

Sustain the orphan and widow

All **and give food to those who hunger.**

Grant them the joy of your help again

All **and sustain them with your Spirit.**

O Lord, judge the peoples

All **and take all nations for your own.**

CWDP

God of infinite mercy,
we trust in your good purposes of peace for all your children.
We pray for those who at this time
face danger in the defence of justice.
Watch over those in peril;
support those who are anxious for loved ones;
gather into your eternal purpose those who will die.
Remove from the hearts of all people
the passions that keep alive the spirit of war,
and in your goodness restore peace among us;
for the sake of the Prince of peace,
Jesus Christ our Lord.

All **Amen.**

BCO

THE CONCLUSION

COMMITMENT

Let us commit ourselves to responsible living and faithful service.

Will you strive for all that makes for peace?

All **We will.**

Will you seek to heal the wounds of war?

All **We will.**

Will you work for a just future for all humanity?

All **We will.**

Lord God our Father,
we pledge ourselves
to serve you and all your peoples,
in the cause of peace,
for the relief of want and suffering,
and for the praise of your name.
Guide us by your Spirit;
give us wisdom;
give us courage;
give us hope;
and keep us faithful
now and always.

All **Amen.**

SR 1968, adapted

NATIONAL ANTHEM

All **God save our gracious Queen,**
Long live our noble Queen,
God save the Queen.
Send her victorious,
Happy and glorious,
Long to reign over us:
God save the Queen.

ENDING

> Go forth into the world in peace;
> be of good courage;
> hold fast that which is good;
> render to no one evil for evil;
> strengthen the faint-hearted;
> support the weak;
> help the afflicted;
> honour everyone;
> love and serve the Lord,
> rejoicing in the power of the Holy Spirit;
>
> and the blessing of God almighty,
> the Father, the Son, and the Holy Spirit,
> be among you and remain with you always.

All   **Amen.**

4 A VETERANS' SERVICE

not held on Remembrance Sunday

A model for use when members of the British Legion, or of an Armed Service or Regimental Association, come to church for a day of celebration and commemoration. This pattern may also be used in any circumstances when it is not necessary, for reasons of time, to begin with the Act of Remembrance.

THE PREPARATION

HYMN

During the singing of this hymn Legion, Association and other standards and flags may be presented and stood in a place of honour in the sanctuary. Regimental colours should be laid upon the holy table.

GREETING

Grace, mercy and peace from God our Father
and the Lord Jesus Christ be with you

All   **and also with you.**

PENITENCE

The minister says

Let us confess to God
the sins and shortcomings of the world;
its pride, its selfishness, its greed;
its evil divisions and hatreds.
Let us confess our share in what is wrong,
and our failure to seek and establish that peace
which God wills for his children.

All   **Most merciful God,**
        we confess that we have sinned
        in thought, word, and deed.
        We have not loved you with our whole heart.
        We have not loved our neighbours as ourselves.
        In your mercy
        forgive what we have been,
        help us to amend what we are,
        and direct what we shall be;
        that we may do justly,
        love mercy,
        and walk humbly with you;
        through Jesus Christ our Lord.
        Amen.

The minister stands and says
        Almighty God, have mercy upon us,
        pardon and deliver us from all our sins,
        confirm and strengthen us in all goodness,
        and keep us in life eternal;
        through Jesus Christ our Lord.

All   **Amen.**

SR 1968

HYMN

THE SERVICE OF THE WORD

OPENING PRAYER

        Almighty God,
        stretch forth your mighty arm
        to strengthen and protect the armed forces:
        grant that meeting danger with courage
        and all occasions with discipline and loyalty,
        they may truly serve the cause of justice and peace;
        to the honour of your holy name,
        through Jesus Christ our Lord.

All   **Amen.**

READING

HYMN

READING

SERMON

HYMN

PRAYERS

*The Lord's Prayer may conclude the prayers, and may be introduced with
these words*

> Gathering our prayers and praises into one,
> let us pray with confidence
> as our Saviour has taught us.

All **Our Father, who art in heaven,
hallowed be thy name;
thy kingdom come;
thy will be done;
on earth as it is in heaven.
Give us this day our daily bread.
And forgive us our trespasses,
as we forgive those who trespass against us.
And lead us not into temptation;
but deliver us from evil.
For thine is the kingdom,
the power, and the glory,
for ever and ever.
Amen.**

THE ACT OF REMEMBRANCE

HYMN

During this hymn the standards should be returned to their bearers who should remain in view of the congregation without obscuring their view of the ministers or the holy table.

REMEMBRANCE

The presiding minister says
>Let us remember before God,
>and commend to his sure keeping:
>those who have died for their country in conflict;
>those whom we knew, and whose memory we treasure;
>and all who have lived and died in the service of humanity.

A second (older) voice says
>They shall grow not old as we that are left grow old:
>Age shall not weary them, nor the years condemn.

A third (younger) voice says
>At the going down of the sun and in the morning
>We will remember them.

All   **We will remember them.**

SR 1968, adapted

The standards are dipped.

>(The Last Post)   The Silence   (The Reveille)

The standards are raised.

KOHIMA EPITAPH

Another voice may say
>When you go home tell them of us and say:
>'For your tomorrow, we gave our today.'

A token wreath may be laid in a prominent place.

The page of a Book of Remembrance may be turned.

The presiding minister says

> Most merciful and ever-living God,
> we remember those whom you have gathered
> from the storm of war into the peace of your presence:
> grant that we, being faithful till death,
> may receive with them the crown of life that never fades,
> through Jesus Christ our Lord.

All   **Amen.**

The prayer of Commemoration may be replaced by a Regimental Collect. Such a collect might also be used as the Opening Prayer or as a Gathering Prayer before or instead of the penitential section. A Regimental Collect with a suitable introduction might replace the prayer of commitment which follows.

THE CONCLUSION

COMMITMENT

> Let us pledge ourselves anew
> to the service of God and humanity:
> that we may help, encourage, and comfort others,
> and support those working for the relief of the needy
> and for the peace and welfare of the nations.

All   **Lord God our Father,**
> **we pledge ourselves**
> **to serve you and all your peoples,**
> **in the cause of peace,**
> **for the relief of want and suffering,**
> **and for the praise of your name.**
> **Guide us by your Spirit;**
> **give us wisdom;**
> **give us courage;**
> **give us hope;**
> **and keep us faithful**
> **now and always.**
> **Amen.**

SR 1968, adapted

NATIONAL ANTHEM

The standards are dipped.

All   **God save our gracious Queen,**
      Long live our noble Queen,
      God save the Queen.
      Send her victorious,
      Happy and glorious,
      Long to reign over us:
      God save the Queen.

      Thy choicest gifts in store
      On her be pleased to pour,
      Long may she reign.
      May she defend our laws,
      And ever give us cause
      To sing with heart and voice,
      God save the Queen.

The standards are raised.

BLESSING

    May the God of all power and might
    make you strong in faith and love,
    defend you on every side,
    and guide you in truth and peace;

    and the blessing of God almighty,
    the Father, the Son, and the Holy Spirit,
    be among you and remain with you always.

All   **Amen.**

HYMN

The standards depart.

The ministers depart.

5 REMEMBRANCE WITHIN A EUCHARISTIC RITE

The Act of Remembrance may be used in three positions in the liturgy, depending on time.

1 *At the start, after or instead of the prayers of penitence. The Remembrance and Commemoration should be said. The Commitment should be used as the Prayer after Communion.*

2 *In the centre of the liturgy, instead of the Prayers of Intercession. In those Rites with a central offering of the Peace, this becomes the natural conclusion of the Remembrance. The Commitment should be used as the Prayer after Communion.*

3 *At the end of the liturgy. The order is as for the Veterans' Service, pages 72–7 above. The Act of Remembrance and the Commitment lead naturally into the conclusion of the whole act of worship.*

The material in Common Worship: Times and Seasons *should be noted.*

6   DIVINE SERVICE – ECUMENICAL STRUCTURE

This order is based on Morning and Evening Prayer and on the Liturgy of the Word from the Holy Eucharist. It is a flexible ecumenical structure upon which to base simple prayers or a formal act of worship. It may be used with or without an Act of Remembrance.

THE GATHERING

A hymn may be sung as the ministers enter.

The presiding minister says
>In the name of the Father,
>and of the Son,
>and of the Holy Spirit.

All   **Amen.**

>Grace, mercy and peace from God our Father
>and the Lord Jesus Christ be with you

All   **and also with you.**

>This is the day that the Lord has made.

All   **Let us rejoice and be glad in it.**

or, especially in the morning
>O Lord, open our lips

All   **and our mouth shall proclaim your praise.**
>Give us the joy of your saving help

All   **and sustain us with your life-giving Spirit.**

or, especially in the evening
>O God, make speed to save us.

All   **O Lord, make haste to help us.**
>Lead your people to freedom, O God.

All   **And banish all darkness from our hearts and minds.**

We have come together in the name of Christ
to offer our praise and thanksgiving,
to hear and receive God's holy word,
to pray for the needs of the world,
(to remember those who have suffered in conflict, war and terror,)
and to seek the forgiveness of our sins,
that by the power of the Holy Spirit
we may give ourselves to the service of God.

A minister says an invitation to confession

Gathered together as God's family,
let us ask forgiveness from our heavenly Father,
for he is full of gentleness and compassion.

All   **Lord God,**
we have sinned against you;
we have done evil in your sight.
We are sorry and repent.
Have mercy on us according to your love.
Wash away our wrongdoing
and cleanse us from our sin.
Renew a right spirit within us
and restore us to the joy of your salvation;
through Jesus Christ our Lord.
Amen.

The presiding minister says this or some other absolution

May the Father of all mercies cleanse *you* from *your* sins,
and restore *you* in his image to the praise and glory of his name,
through Jesus Christ our Lord.

All   **Amen.**

These words may be used.

Holy God, holy and mighty, holy and immortal:
have mercy upon us.

All   **Holy God, holy and mighty, holy and immortal:**
have mercy upon us.

THE COLLECT

The presiding minister says the Opening Prayer or Collect, and all respond

All **Amen.**

THE LITURGY OF THE WORD

One or two readings follow.
After each reading these words may be used.

This is the word of the Lord.

All **Thanks be to God.**

A psalm, canticle or hymn may be sung.

The Gospel may be read formally, especially at a principal morning service. An acclamation may herald the Gospel reading.
All remain standing.

Hear the Gospel of our Lord Jesus Christ according to N.

All **Glory to you, O Lord.**

At the end

This is the Gospel of the Lord.

All **Praise to you, O Christ.**

THE SERMON

A hymn may be sung.

All   **I believe in God, the Father almighty,**
creator of heaven and earth.

I believe in Jesus Christ, his only Son, our Lord,
who was conceived by the Holy Spirit,
born of the Virgin Mary,
suffered under Pontius Pilate,
was crucified, died, and was buried;
he descended to the dead.
On the third day he rose again;
he ascended into heaven,
he is seated at the right hand of the Father,
and he will come to judge the living and the dead.

I believe in the Holy Spirit,
the holy catholic Church,
the communion of saints,
the forgiveness of sins,
the resurrection of the body,
and the life everlasting.
Amen.

PRAYERS OF INTERCESSION

The presiding minister may begin the prayers of intercession
In the power of the Spirit,
and in union with Christ
let us pray to the Father.

The ministers and others may introduce biddings.

Any of these responses may be used.

Lord, in your mercy
All **hear our prayer.**

Lord, hear us.
All **Lord, graciously hear us.**

Let us pray to the Lord:
All **Lord, have mercy.**

The intercessions may end
Merciful Father,
All **accept these prayers**
for the sake of your Son,
our Saviour Jesus Christ.
Amen.

Or else the presiding minister may use this or another concluding prayer
Heavenly Father,
you have promised through your Son Jesus Christ,
that when we meet in his name,
and pray according to his mind,
he will be among us and hear our prayer:
in your love and mercy fulfil our desires,
and give us your greatest gift,
which is to know you, the only true God,
and your Son Jesus Christ our Lord.
All **Amen.**

Or if an Act of Remembrance is to follow, the Lord's Prayer may conclude the intercessions.

The Lord's Prayer is introduced
Gathering our prayers and praises into one,
let us pray with confidence
as our Saviour has taught us.

All **Our Father ...**

THE ACT OF REMEMBRANCE

HYMN

During this hymn the standards should be returned to their bearers who should remain in view of the congregation without obscuring their view of the ministers or the holy table.

REMEMBRANCE

The presiding minister says
> Let us remember before God,
> and commend to his sure keeping:
> those who have died for their country in conflict;
> those whom we knew, and whose memory we treasure;
> and all who have lived and died in the service of humanity.

A second (older) voice says
> They shall grow not old as we that are left grow old:
> Age shall not weary them, nor the years condemn.

A third (younger) voice says
> At the going down of the sun and in the morning
> We will remember them.

All   **We will remember them.**

SR 1968, adapted

> *The standards are dipped.*

> *(The Last Post)*   *The Silence*   *(The Reveille)*

The standards are raised.

KOHIMA EPITAPH

Another voice may say
> When you go home tell them of us and say:
> 'For your tomorrow, we gave our today.'

A token wreath may be laid in a prominent place.

The page of a Book of Remembrance may be turned.

Most merciful and ever-living God,
we remember those whom you have gathered
from the storm of war into the peace of your presence:
grant that we, being faithful till death,
may receive with them the crown of life that never fades,
through Jesus Christ our Lord.

All **Amen.**

The prayer of Commemoration may be replaced by a Regimental Collect. Such a collect might also be used as the Opening Prayer or as a Gathering Prayer before or instead of the penitential section. A Regimental Collect with a suitable intro-duction might replace the prayer of commitment which follows.

THE CONCLUSION

COMMITMENT

Let us pledge ourselves anew
to the service of God and humanity:
that we may help, encourage, and comfort others,
and support those working for the relief of the needy
and for the peace and welfare of the nations.

All **Lord God our Father,
we pledge ourselves
to serve you and all your peoples,
in the cause of peace,
for the relief of want and suffering,
and for the praise of your name.
Guide us by your Spirit;
give us wisdom;
give us courage;
give us hope;
and keep us faithful
now and always.
Amen.**

SR 1968, adapted

The standards are dipped.

All **God save our gracious Queen,**
Long live our noble Queen,
God save the Queen.
Send her victorious,
Happy and glorious,
Long to reign over us:
God save the Queen.

The standards are raised.

BLESSING

May the God of all power and might
make you strong in faith and love,
defend you on every side,
and guide you in truth and peace;

and the blessing of God almighty,
the Father, the Son, and the Holy Spirit,
be among you and remain with you always.

All **Amen.**

HYMN

The standards depart.

The ministers depart.

THE CONCLUSION
WITHOUT AN ACT OF REMEMBRANCE

A hymn may be sung.
A collection may be taken.

The Lord's Prayer is introduced
> Gathering our prayers and praises into one,
> let us pray with confidence
> as our Saviour has taught us.

All **Our Father, who art in heaven,**
hallowed be thy name;
thy kingdom come;
thy will be done;
on earth as it is in heaven.
Give us this day our daily bread.
And forgive us our trespasses,
as we forgive those who trespass against us.
And lead us not into temptation;
but deliver us from evil.
For thine is the kingdom,
the power, and the glory,
for ever and ever.
Amen.

This reponsory may be used.
> Make your ways known upon the earth, Lord God,
All **your saving power among all peoples.**

> Renew your Church in holiness
All **and help us serve you with joy.**

> Guide the leaders of this and every nation,
All **that justice may prevail throughout the world.**

> Let not the needy be forgotten,
All **nor the hope of the poor be taken away.**

> Make us instruments of your peace
All **and let your glory be over all the earth.**

A Regimental, Corps or Service Collect or another specific formal prayer may be
used, and the following prayer may be said by all.

All   **Almighty God,**
we thank you for the gift of your holy word.
May it be a lantern to our feet,
a light to our paths,
and a strength to our lives.
Take us and use us
to love and serve
in the power of the Holy Spirit
and in the name of your Son,
Jesus Christ our Lord.
Amen.

The service ends with one of the following

The Lord be with you
All   **and also with you.**

Let us bless the Lord.
All   **Thanks be to God.**

The Lord bless us,
and preserve us from all evil,
and keep us in eternal life.
All   **Amen.**

or

All   **The grace of our Lord Jesus Christ,**
and the love of God,
and the fellowship of the Holy Spirit,
be with us all evermore.
Amen.

Or the presiding minister may say a blessing, to which all respond
All   **Amen.**

A hymn may be sung.

The ministers depart.

This is not an example of a Service for Remembrancetide, but will help those at home to pray for troops in danger, and to remember those who may have recently fallen.

PREPARATION

> O God, make speed to save us.

All **O Lord, make haste to help us.**

or

> I lift up my eyes to the hills;
> from where is my help to come?
> My help comes from the Lord,
> the maker of heaven and earth.

Psalm 121.1–2

PRAISE

This canticle may be used, or else a hymn.

Great and Wonderful

> Great and wonderful are your deeds,
> Lord God the Almighty.

All **Just and true are your ways,**
O ruler of the nations.

> Who shall not revere and praise your name, O Lord?
> For you alone are holy.

All **All nations shall come and worship in your presence:**
for your just dealings have been revealed.

Revelation 15.3–4

> To the One who sits on the throne and to the Lamb
> be blessing and honour and glory and might,
>   for ever and ever. Amen.

CW

Almighty God,
stretch forth your mighty arm
to strengthen and protect the armed forces:
grant that meeting danger with courage
and all occasions with discipline and loyalty,
they may truly serve the cause of justice and peace;
to the honour of your holy name,
through Jesus Christ our Lord.

All **Amen.**

THE WORD OF GOD

Seek good and not evil,
    that you may live;
and so the Lord, the God of hosts, will be with you,
    just as you have said.
Hate evil and love good,
    and establish justice in the gate;
it may be that the Lord, the God of hosts,
    will be gracious to the remnant of Joseph.

Amos 5.14–15

or

We are afflicted in every way, but not crushed; perplexed, but not
driven to despair; persecuted, but not forsaken; struck down, but
not destroyed; always carrying in the body the death of Jesus, so that
the life of Jesus may also be made visible in our bodies.

2 Corinthians 4.8–10

or

Be strong in the Lord and in the strength of his power. Put on the whole armour of God, so that you may be able to stand against the wiles of the devil. For our struggle is not against enemies of blood and flesh, but against the rulers, against the authorities, against the cosmic powers of this present darkness, against the spiritual forces of evil in the heavenly places. Therefore take up the whole armour of God, so that you may be able to withstand on that evil day, and having done everything, to stand firm. Stand therefore, and fasten the belt of truth around your waist, and put on the breastplate of righteousness. As shoes for your feet put on whatever will make you ready to proclaim the gospel of peace. With all of these, take the shield of faith, with which you will be able to quench all the flaming arrows of the evil one. Take the helmet of salvation, and the sword of the Spirit, which is the word of God. Pray in the Spirit at all times in every prayer and supplication. To that end keep alert and always persevere in supplication for all the saints.

Ephesians 6.10–18

or

God so loved the world that he gave his only Son, so that every-one who believes in him may not perish but may have eternal life. Indeed, God did not send the Son into the world to condemn the world, but in order that the world might be saved through him.

John 3.16–17

In peace let us pray to the Lord.

For the people of God,
that they may worship you in spirit and in truth,
let us pray to the Lord:

All   **Lord, have mercy.**

For the leaders of the nations,
that you will guide them in the ways of justice, mercy and truth,
let us pray to the Lord:

All   **Lord, have mercy.**

For the peacemakers, that you may protect them from all evil,
let us pray to the Lord:

All   **Lord, have mercy.**

For our loved ones, wherever they may be
and for those who wear the Queen's uniform on our behalf,
let us pray to the Lord:

All   **Lord, have mercy.**

For our enemies, and those who wish us harm,
that you may turn the hearts of all to kindness and friendship,
let us pray to the Lord:

All   **Lord, have mercy.**

For the sick and wounded,
and for all prisoners and captives,
that they may know your power to heal and save,
let us pray to the Lord:

All   **Lord, have mercy.**

BE

Almighty God,
you see that we have no power of ourselves to help ourselves:
keep us both outwardly in our bodies,
and inwardly in our souls;
that we may be defended from all adversities
    which may happen to the body,
and from all evil thoughts which may assault and hurt the soul;
through Jesus Christ our Lord.

All   **Amen.**

But if there have been fatalities the above prayer is omitted, and the litany continued into an Act of Remembrance

>For those who mourn ...
>let us pray to the Lord:

All **Lord, have mercy.**

>For those who have died in the conflict ...
>let us pray to the Lord:

All **Lord, have mercy.**

BE

>They shall grow not old as we that are left grow old:
>Age shall not weary them, nor the years condemn.
>At the going down of the sun and in the morning
>We will remember them.

All **We will remember them.**

>*(The Last Post)*   *The Silence*   *(The Reveille)*

>Most merciful and ever-living God,
>we remember those whom you have gathered
>from the storm of war into the peace of your presence:
>grant that we, being faithful till death,
>may receive with them the crown of life that never fades,
>through Jesus Christ our Lord.

All **Amen.**

Free prayer may be offered and may include these concerns:

>*those in authority, for the right use of power*
>*those who bear arms, for discipline, discernment and compassion*
>*victims and perpetrators of violence, for healing and repentance*

The Lord's Prayer is said

Gathering our prayers and praises into one,
let us pray with confidence
as our Saviour has taught us.

All **Our Father, who art in heaven,
hallowed be thy name;
thy kingdom come;
thy will be done;
on earth as it is in heaven.
Give us this day our daily bread.
And forgive us our trespasses,
as we forgive those who trespass against us.
And lead us not into temptation;
but deliver us from evil.
For thine is the kingdom,
the power, and the glory,
for ever and ever.
Amen.**

PRAYER FOR THE SAFETY OF TROOPS

A hymn may be sung, and this part of Psalm 27 may be said
The Lord is my light and my salvation;
whom then shall I fear?

All **The Lord is the strength of my life;
of whom then shall I be afraid?**

When the wicked, even my enemies and my foes,
came upon me to eat up my flesh,
they stumbled and fell.

All **Though a host encamp against me,
my heart shall not be afraid,**

and though there rise up war against me,
yet will I put my trust in him.

All **For in the day of trouble
he shall hide me in his shelter;**

in the secret place of his dwelling shall he hide me
and set me high upon a rock.

Psalm 27. 1–3, 6

This prayer shall be said

> Let us pray to the Lord for the safety of our troops.

> May the cross of the Son of God,
> which is mightier than all the hosts of Satan
> and more glorious than all the hosts of heaven,
> abide with them in their going out and their coming in.
> By day and by night, at morning and at evening,
> at all times and in all places may it protect and defend them.
> From the wrath of evildoers, from the assaults of evil spirits,
> from foes visible and invisible, from the snares of the devil,
> from all passions that beguile the soul and body:
> may it guard, protect and deliver them.

All **Amen.**

Christaraksha, an Indian Prayer

THE CONCLUSION

After a silence, a time-of-day prayer may be said before the final prayer.

Morning

> Almighty and everlasting God,
> we thank you that you have brought us safely
> to the beginning of this day.
> Keep us from falling into sin
> or running into danger,
> order us in all our doings
> and guide us to do always
> what is righteous in your sight;
> through Jesus Christ our Lord.

All **Amen.**

BCP

Daytime

> God of love and compassion,
> your grace is all we need this day:
> give us the wisdom to know what is true,
> and the courage to do what is right;
> be with us in time of danger,
> and show us the way to peace;
> through Jesus Christ our Lord.

All **Amen.**

BE

    Lighten our darkness,
    Lord, we pray,
    and in your great mercy
    defend us from all perils and dangers of this night,
    for the love of your only Son,
    our Saviour Jesus Christ

All   **Amen.**

BCP

Night

    Keep watch, dear Lord,
    with those who wake, or watch, or weep this night,
    and give your angels charge over those who sleep.
    Tend the sick,
    give rest to the weary,
    sustain the dying,
    calm the suffering,
    and pity the distressed;
    all for your love's sake,
    O Christ our Redeemer.

All   **Amen.**

Augustine of Hippo (354–430)

Final Prayer

    May the Lord bless us,
    may he deliver us from all evil,
    and keep us in life eternal.

All   **Amen.**

8   SERVICE OF PRAYER FOR HEALING AND STRENGTH

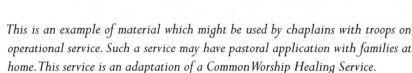

This is an example of material which might be used by chaplains with troops on operational service. Such a service may have pastoral application with families at home. This service is an adaptation of a Common Worship Healing Service.

INTRODUCTION

When pursued in defence of the poor and helpless, and for the promotion of peace and justice, the profession of arms is noble; but those who bear arms expose both their bodies and souls to extraordinary risks. Those in battle may see and do such awful deeds that afterwards they may not be able to quieten their consciences. Those preparing for battle would not be fit for armed service in our society if they were not apprehensive of what might be required of them. Although this 'Strengthening Service' may be used at any time, it is primarily for use before or after engaging hostile forces: it is a prayer 'that we may be defended from all adversities which may happen to the body, and from all evil thoughts which may assault and hurt the soul'. After the Word of God has been heard, and prayers said for his protection and peace, the ancient ceremonies of the laying on of hands and of the anointing with holy oils are offered. The laying on of hands may be done in the absence of a chaplain, and is a way of sharing hurt and understandable anxiety with each other and the Lord. The anointing with holy oil requires a chaplain or other authorized lay minister. In both ceremonies, which are optional for all, we ask the Lord of all peace to fill us with his blessing; to protect us from all evil; and to forgive us for what we have done, or may have to do, or have failed to prevent.

After these ceremonies should any person have a conscience that remains troubled a chaplain should be approached in confidence. The order of Reconciliation (Confession) may then be used.

BE

Bless the Lord, O my soul;
All **and forget not all his benefits.**

God forgives all our iniquities;
All **and heals all our weaknesses.**

God redeems our life from the Pit;
All **and crowns us with love and mercy.**

Blessed are you, sovereign God, gentle and merciful,
creator of heaven and earth.
Your word brought light out of darkness.
In Jesus Christ you proclaim good news to the poor,
liberty to captives, sight to the blind
and freedom for the oppressed.
Daily your Spirit renews the face of the earth,
bringing life and health, justice and mercy, wholeness and peace.
In the renewal of our lives
you make known your heavenly glory.
Blessed be God, Father, Son and Holy Spirit:
All **Blessed be God for ever.**

THE COLLECT

Almighty God,
you see that we have no power of ourselves to help ourselves:
keep us both outwardly in our bodies,
and inwardly in our souls;
that we may be defended from all adversities
    which may happen to the body,
and from all evil thoughts which may assault and hurt the soul;
through Jesus Christ our Lord.
All **Amen.**

CW

One or more readings follow as time and circumstances permit.

Psalm 91 may be said, or a hymn may be sung.

All **Keep us, good Lord, under the shadow of your mercy.**

> Whoever dwells in the shelter of the Most High
> and abides under the shadow of the Almighty,
> Shall say to the Lord, 'My refuge and my stronghold,
> my God, in whom I put my trust.'

All **Keep us, good Lord, under the shadow of your mercy.**

> You shall not be afraid of any terror by night,
> nor of the arrow that flies by day;
> Of the pestilence that stalks in darkness,
> nor of the sickness that destroys at noonday.
> Though a thousand fall at your side
> and ten thousand at your right hand,
> yet it shall not come near you.
> Your eyes have only to behold
> to see the reward of the wicked.

All **Keep us, good Lord, under the shadow of your mercy.**

> Because you have made the Lord your refuge
> and the Most High your stronghold,
> there shall no evil happen to you,
> neither shall any plague come near your tent.
> For he shall give his angels charge over you,
> to keep you in all your ways.
> They shall bear you in their hands,
> lest you dash your foot against a stone.

All **Keep us, good Lord, under the shadow of your mercy.**

Psalm 91.1–2,5–12

This psalm prayer may be said

> Keep us, good Lord,
> under the shadow of your mercy
> and, as you have bound us to yourself in love,
> leave us not who call upon your name,
> and grant us your salvation,
> made known in Jesus Christ our Lord.

All **Amen.**

CWDPP

The whole armour of God

Be strong in the Lord and in the strength of his power. Put on the whole armour of God, so that you may be able to stand against the wiles of the devil. For our struggle is not against enemies of blood and flesh, but against the rulers, against the authorities, against the cosmic powers of this present darkness, against the spiritual forces of evil in the heavenly places. Therefore take up the whole armour of God, so that you may be able to withstand on that evil day, and having done everything, to stand firm. Stand therefore, and fasten the belt of truth around your waist, and put on the breastplate of righteousness. As shoes for your feet put on whatever will make you ready to proclaim the gospel of peace. With all of these, take the shield of faith, with which you will be able to quench all the flaming arrows of the evil one. Take the helmet of salvation, and the sword of the Spirit, which is the word of God. Pray in the Spirit at all times in every prayer and supplication. To that end keep alert and always persevere in supplication for all the saints.

Ephesians 6.10–18

By Christ's wounds you have been healed

For it is a credit to you if, being aware of God, you endure pain while suffering unjustly. If you endure when you are beaten for doing wrong, what credit is that? But if you endure when you do right and suffer for it, you have God's approval. For to this you have been called, because Christ also suffered for you, leaving you an example, so that you should follow in his steps. 'He committed no sin, and no deceit was found in his mouth.' When he was abused, he did not return abuse; when he suffered, he did not threaten; but he entrusted himself to the one who judges justly. He himself bore our sins in his body on the cross, so that, free from sins, we might live for righteousness; by his wounds you have been healed. For you were going astray like sheep, but now you have returned to the shepherd and guardian of your souls.

1 Peter 2.19–end

If Holy Communion is celebrated as part of this service, one of these or some other Gospel reading shall be used:

Serving Christ in others	*Matthew 25.34–40*
The Sermon on the Mount	*Matthew 5.1–12*
Love your enemies and pray for them	*Matthew 5.43–48*
The Roman soldier	*Matthew 8.5–10*
Do not worry about your life	*Luke 12.4–7, 22–31*
No one has greater love than this	*John 15.9–14*

SERMON

PRAYERS

Holy God, the protector of all who trust in you:
Grant to [N and] all who seek you,
the assurance of your presence,
your power, and your peace.
Lord, hear us.

All **Lord, graciously hear us.**

Grant your healing grace to [N and] all who are sick or wounded,
that they may be made whole in body, mind and spirit.
Lord, hear us.

All **Lord, graciously hear us.**

Be with all medics and chaplains,
and all who support the suffering:
give them wisdom and skill, sympathy and patience.
Lord, hear us.

All **Lord, graciously hear us.**

[Receive [our comrade(s) N and N and] all those who have fallen;
show mercy to their loved ones at home.
Lord, hear us.

All **Lord, graciously hear us.]**

Sustain and support the anxious and fearful
and renew them with courage from on high.
Lord, hear us.

All **Lord, graciously hear us.**

Comfort our loved ones, anxious at home,
surround them with your love,
and protect them from all harm.
Lord, hear us.

All **Lord, graciously hear us.**

Give wisdom to our leaders and commanders,
that we may be a force for good in *the land / these waters*.
Lord, hear us.

All **Lord, graciously hear us.**

Be with all who defend your truth and your peace:
that we may vanquish injustice and wrong.
Lord, hear us.

All **Lord, graciously hear us.**

Bring healing and wholeness to people and nations:
let your justice rule our hearts,
and your mercy our actions.
Lord, hear us.

All **Lord, graciously hear us**.

BE

Lord our God, our sure stronghold,
hear the voice of our pleading
and deliver us from every evil.
Strengthen us as we strive for the poor and oppressed,
and establish your justice in all the earth.

All **Amen.**

CWDPP, Psalm 140

THE MINISTRY OF HEALING

The Ministry of Healing may take place here using these or other suitable prayers. These ceremonies may be omitted, and the service concluded as printed. Holy Communion may be administered 'by extension'.

Be with us, Spirit of God;

All   **nothing can separate us from your love.**

Breathe on us, breath of God;

All   **fill us with your saving power.**

Speak in us, wisdom of God;

All   **bring strength, healing and peace.**

Silence is kept.

When anointing, a chaplain may use this prayer over the olive oil, if it has not previously been blessed.

Lord, holy Father, giver of health and salvation,
as your apostles anointed those who were sick and healed them,
so continue the ministry of healing in your Church.
Sanctify this oil, that those who are anointed with it
may be freed from suffering and distress,
find inward peace, and know the joy of your salvation,
through your Son, our Saviour Jesus Christ.

All   **Amen.**

The laying on of hands may be administered with these words

In the name of God and trusting in his might alone,
receive Christ's healing touch to make you whole.
May Christ bring you wholeness of body, mind and spirit,
deliver you from every evil,
and give you his peace.

All   **Amen.**

When anointing, a chaplain or other authorized minister may use these words
　　N, I anoint you in the name of God who gives you life.
　　Receive Christ's forgiveness, his healing and his love.
　　May the Father of our Lord Jesus Christ
　　grant you the riches of his grace,
　　his wholeness and his peace.

All　**Amen.**

This prayer concludes the Ministry of Healing
　　Lord God, our protector and guide,
　　who made us knowing both good and evil:
　　receive our prayer and, by your wisdom,
　　help us to discern and desire all that is good,
　　that the offering of our lives may be a service acceptable to you;
　　through Jesus Christ,
　　who suffered the darkness of torment and trial
　　and now is alive and reigns with you and the Holy Spirit,
　　for ever and ever.

All　**Amen.**

CWDPP, Psalm 141

THE CONCLUSION

A hymn may be sung, and this part of Psalm 27 may be said

The Lord is my light and my salvation;
whom then shall I fear?

All **The Lord is the strength of my life;**
of whom then shall I be afraid?

When the wicked, even my enemies and my foes,
came upon me to eat up my flesh,
they stumbled and fell.

All **Though a host encamp against me,**
my heart shall not be afraid,

and though there rise up war against me,
yet will I put my trust in him.

All **For in the day of trouble**
he shall hide me in his shelter;

in the secret place of his dwelling shall he hide me
and set me high upon a rock.

Psalm 27.1–3,6

Final Collect

O God our deliverer,
defender of the poor and needy:
when the foundations of the earth are shaking
give strength to your people
to uphold justice and fight all wrong
in the name of you Son,
Jesus Christ our Lord.

All **Amen.**

CWDPP, Psalm 82

The Lord's Prayer

Let us pray with confidence as our Saviour has taught us

All   **Our Father, who art in heaven ...**

Peace to you from God our Father who hears our cry.
Peace from his Son Jesus Christ whose death brings healing.
Peace from the Holy Spirit who gives us life and strength.

The peace of the Lord be always with you
All   **and also with you.**

A chaplain may add this Blessing
Go forth into the world in peace;
be of good courage;
hold fast that which is good;
render to no one evil for evil;
strengthen the faint-hearted;
support the weak;
help the afflicted;
honour everyone;
love and serve the Lord,
rejoicing in the power of the Holy Spirit;

and the blessing of God almighty,
the Father, the Son, and the Holy Spirit,
be among you and remain with you always.
All   **Amen.**

NATIONAL

OFFICIAL

RESOURCES

THE SERVICE OF REMEMBRANCE 1968 / 1984 (SPCK)

Remembrance Sunday is observed on the second Sunday in November, which is the Sunday nearest to 11 November.

Since 1968, a Service for Remembrance Sunday has been commended for general use by the Archbishops of Canterbury, of York, and of Wales, the Cardinal Arch-bishop of Westminster, and the Moderator of the Free Church Federal Council. This service was reissued in 1984 with modest updating of the language and a fresh choice of hymns. The 1984 text, as published in The Promise of His Glory, *is set out below.*

All stand while the minister reads

1 THE INTRODUCTION

>   We are here to worship Almighty God,
>   whose purposes are good;
>   whose power sustains the world he has made;
>   who loves us, though we have failed in his service;
>   who gave Jesus Christ for the life of the world;
>   who by his Holy Spirit leads us in his way.
>   As we give thanks for his great works,
>   we remember those who have lived and died
>   in his service and in the service of others;
>   we pray for all who suffer through war and are in need;
>   we ask for his help and blessing that we may do his will,
>   and that the whole world may acknowledge him as Lord and King.

2 HYMN

3 LESSON

4 HYMN

5 ACT OF PENITENCE

The minister says

>Let us confess to God
>the sins and shortcomings of the world;
>its pride, its selfishness, its greed;
>its evil divisions and hatreds.
>Let us confess our share in what is wrong,
>and our failure to seek and establish that peace
>which God wills for his children.

After a short silence, all say

All   **Most merciful God,**
>**we confess that we have sinned**
>**in thought, word, and deed.**
>**We have not loved you with our whole heart.**
>**We have not loved our neighbours as ourselves.**
>**In your mercy**
>**forgive what we have been,**
>**help us to amend what we are,**
>**and direct what we shall be;**
>**that we may do justly, love mercy,**
>**and walk humbly with you;**
>**through Jesus Christ our Lord.**
>**Amen.**

The minister stands and says

>Almighty God, have mercy upon us,
>pardon and deliver us from all our sins,
>confirm and strengthen us in all goodness,
>and keep us in life eternal;
>through Jesus Christ our Lord.

All   **Amen.**

6 INTERCESSION

Special intentions may be inserted at appropriate points.

The minister says

Let us pray for the peace of the world:
for statesmen and rulers,
that they may have wisdom to know and courage to do
    what is right ...

for all who work to improve international relationships,
that they may find the true way
to reconcile people of different race, colour, and creed ...

and for men and women the world over,
that they may have justice and freedom,
and live in security and peace ...

Here follows a short silence.

Lord, in your mercy

All **hear our prayer.**

Most gracious God and Father,
in whose will is our peace:
turn our hearts and the hearts of all to yourself,
that by the power of your Spirit
the peace which is founded on righteousness
may be established throughout the whole world;
through Jesus Christ our Lord.

All **Amen.**

Let us pray for all who suffer as a result of war:
for the injured and the disabled,
for the mentally distressed,
and for those whose faith in God and man has been
weakened or destroyed ...

for the homeless and refugees,
for those who are hungry,
and for all who have lost their livelihood and security ...

for those who mourn their dead,
those who have lost husband or wife,
children or parents,
and especially for those who have no hope in Christ
to sustain them in their grief ...

Here follows a short silence.

Lord, in your mercy
All **hear our prayer.**

Almighty God, our heavenly Father,
infinite in wisdom, love, and power:
have compassion on those for whom we pray;
and help us to use all suffering
in the cause of your kingdom;
through him who gave himself for us on the cross,
Jesus Christ your Son, our Lord.
All **Amen.**

If there is a collection, it is taken during the hymn which follows.

7 HYMN

8 SERMON

9 HYMN

10 ACT OF REMEMBRANCE

All stand while the minister says
Let us remember before God,
and commend to his sure keeping
those who have died for their country in war;
those whom we knew, and whose memory we treasure;
and all who have lived and died
in the service of mankind.

Here follows **The Silence.**

Then the minister says

Almighty and eternal God,
from whose love in Christ we cannot be parted,
either by death or life:
hear our prayers and thanksgivings
for all whom we remember this day;
fulfil in them the purpose of your love;
and bring us all, with them, to your eternal joy;
through Jesus Christ our Lord.

All **Amen.**

11 ACT OF COMMITMENT

The minister, or some other person appointed, says

Let us pledge ourselves anew to the service of God
and our fellow men and women:
that we may help, encourage, and comfort others,
and support those working for the relief of the needy
and for the peace and welfare of the nations.

All say together

All **Lord God our Father,**
we pledge ourselves
to serve you and all mankind,
in the cause of peace,
for the relief of want and suffering,
and for the praise of your name.
Guide us by your Spirit;
give us wisdom;
give us courage;
give us hope;
and keep us faithful
now and always.
Amen.

12 THE LORD'S PRAYER

13 NATIONAL ANTHEM

14 BLESSING

This order has been prepared for use at any time on Remembrance Sunday, not necessarily when the Two Minutes Silence is observed. If it is used in the morning it can be so timed that the Act of Remembrance is reached at 11 a.m. without any alteration of the order. Alternatively, the Act of Remembrance may be taken out of the order and used first at 11 a.m. followed by the rest of the service. Where a brief observance is required, as at a war memorial, the Act of Remembrance may be used, followed by the Act of Commitment, the Lord's Prayer, and the Blessing. If desired, the Act of Remembrance may take the form printed below.

ACT OF REMEMBRANCE (ALTERNATIVE FORM)

All stand while the minister says
>Let us remember before God,
>and commend to his sure keeping:
>>those who have died for their country in war;
>>those whom we knew, and whose memory we treasure;
>>and all who have lived and died
>>in the service of mankind.

The list of those to be remembered by name may then be read.

Then may be said
>They shall grow not old as we that are left grow old:
>Age shall not weary them, nor the years condemn.
>At the going down of the sun and in the morning
>We will remember them.

All **We will remember them.**

*Here follows **The Silence**.*

Then the Last Post and the Reveille may be sounded.

Then the minister says

Almighty and eternal God,
from whose love in Christ we cannot be parted,
either by death or life:
Hear our prayers and thanksgivings
for all whom we remember this day;
fulfil in them the purpose of your love;
and bring us all, with them, to your eternal joy;
through Jesus Christ our Lord.

All **Amen.**

SUPPLEMENTARY TEXTS

This Thanksgiving may be used.

We offer to almighty God
our thanksgiving for the many blessings
with which he has enriched our lives.
For the Queen and her family,
and all who under her bear the responsibility of government:

All **Thanks be to God.**

For those who serve in the Armed Forces of the Crown
on sea and land and in the air:

All **Thanks be to God.**

For doctors, nurses, chaplains,
and all who minister to those in need or distress:

All **Thanks be to God.**

For the unity of our people within the Commonwealth:

All **Thanks be to God.**

For the sacrifices made, especially in two world wars,
whereby our peace has been preserved:

All **Thanks be to God.**

For the Royal British Legion:

All **Thanks be to God.**

This Blessing may be used.

> God grant to the living, grace;
> to the departed, rest;
> to the Church, the Queen, the Commonwealth, and all mankind,
>   peace and concord;
> and to us and all his servants, life everlasting;
> and the blessing of God almighty,
> Father, Son, and Holy Spirit,
> come down upon you and remain with you always.

All **Amen.**

SUPPLEMENTARY TEXT

The National Anthem may be sung in the following form.

All **God save our gracious Queen,**
Long live our noble Queen,
God save the Queen.
Send her victorious,
Happy and glorious,
Long to reign over us:
God save the Queen.

Thy choicest gifts in store
on her be pleased to pour,
Long may she reign.
May she defend our laws,
And ever give us cause
To sing with heart and voice,
God save the Queen.

Not on this land alone –
But be God's mercies known
From shore to shore.
Lord, make the nations see
That men should brothers be,
And form one family
The wide world o'er.

Service for Remembrance Sunday © SPCK 1968, 1984 for the compilers

THE SERVICE OF REMEMBRANCE
from the Book of Common Order of the Church of Scotland 1996

1 to 10 in the first section may be used where a separate Act of Remembrance is held at a war memorial outwith the church.

AT THE WAR MEMORIAL

1 SCRIPTURE SENTENCES

The minister says
> The grace of the Lord Jesus Christ
> be with you.

1 Corinthians 16.23

> Our help is in the name of the Lord,
> maker of heaven and earth.

Psalm 124.8

2 PRAYERS

The minister says
> Let us pray.

> Most gracious God, Father of all mercies,
> we offer our thanks
> for the bounty of your providence
> and the renewing liberty of your grace.
> We rejoice in our inheritance in holy things,
> and in the freedom and peace in which we live.
> Especially on this day we give thanks
> for the remembrance
> we are privileged to make
> of those companions of our way
> whose lives were given in time of war
> (*whose names are written here*).

3 THE TRYST

The minister says

> They shall grow not old,
> as we that are left grow old;
> Age shall not weary them,
> nor the years condemn.
> At the going down of the sun
> and in the morning,
> We will remember them.

All **We will remember them.**

[4 THE LAST POST]

[5 LAMENT]

6 THE SILENCE

Silence is kept for two minutes.

[7 REVEILLE]

8 PRAYERS

The minister says

> Let us in honesty of heart
> seek the Lord's renewing grace,
> to deepen our wisdom and our peace,
> and to equip us as instruments of his kindness.

> Let us pray.

> God of goodness and truth,
> we offer our broken spirits for your healing,
> our searching for your guiding light;
> through Jesus Christ our Lord.

God of light and love,
you desire that all your people
should live in your peace.
Grant us the humility to seek your forgiveness
and the will to practise it
in our dealings with others.

Help us in days to come
to seek the good of the world,
to work for the increase of peace and justice,
and to show tolerance and open-mindedness
towards those whose character and customs
differ from ours.

Grant that our remembrance this day
may be consecrated for practical service,
and the world made better
for our children's children.

Receive our prayers
for the well-being of all people,
especially those who mourn and are sad,
and for all in distress,
both known to us and unknown.
and oppressed people everywhere.

Hear us for the peace of the world,
for the wise resolution of conflicts,
and the release of captive
Grant that the people of the world
may do your will and live in your spirit;
through Jesus Christ our Lord.

All **Amen.**

All **Our Father ...**

9 LAYING OF THE WREATHS

10 BLESSING

IN THE CHURCH

1 CALL TO WORSHIP

The minister says
>We are met this day
>to glorify God whose power sustains the world;
>to remember with thanksgiving
>those who lived and died
>in the service of our country;
>and to ask for God's help and blessing,
>that we may be worthy of their sacrifice
>each day of our life.
>
>Let us worship God.

2 SENTENCES

The minister says
>God is our refuge and our stronghold,
>a timely help in trouble.

Psalm 46.1

>Those who look to the Lord
>will win new strength,
>they will soar as on eagles' wings;
>they will run and not feel faint,
>march on and not grow weary.

Isaiah 40.31

3 HYMN

4 PRAYERS

The minister says

Let us pray.

Eternal God,
you are the shepherd of our souls,
the giver of life everlasting.

On this day
when we commemorate and commend to you
those who lived and died
in the service of others,
we are glad to remember
that your purposes for us are good,
that you gave Jesus Christ
for the life of the world,
and that you lead us by his Holy Spirit
into the paths of righteousness and peace.

Merciful and faithful God,
your purpose is to fold both earth and heaven
in a single peace.

With sorrow we confess
that in our hearts we keep alive
the passions and pride
that lead to hatred and to war.
We are not worthy of your love,
nor of the sacrifice made by others on our behalf.

Lord, have mercy.

All **Christ, have mercy.**

Lord, have mercy.

Almighty God,
pardon and deliver us from all our sins,
confirm and strengthen us in all goodness,
and keep us in life eternal;
through Jesus Christ our Lord.

All **Amen.**

God of unbounded grace,
you declared your reconciling love and power
in the death and resurrection
of our Saviour Jesus Christ.
Teach us, who live only in your forgiveness,
to forgive one another.
Heal our divisions,
cast out our fears,
renew our faith in your unchanging purpose
of goodwill and peace on earth;
through Jesus Christ our Lord,
who lives and reigns
with you and the Holy Spirit,
one God, now and for ever.

All **Amen.**

5 CALL TO REMEMBRANCE

The minister says

Will the congregation please stand.

All or part of the following may be said

Let us remember the kindness of God,
and his favour to us in our time of need.

Let us remember the courage,
devotion to duty,
and the self-sacrifice
of the men and women in our armed forces;
the toil, endurance, and suffering
of those who were not in uniform;
the support of those who sent us help from afar,
or came and stood by our side.

Let us remember those
who were wounded in the fight;
those who perished in air-raids at home;
those who fell in battle,
and are buried at sea
or in some corner of a foreign field;
and especially those
whom we have known and loved,
whose place is for ever in our hearts.

Let us remember those who were our enemies,
whose homes and hearts are as bereft as ours,
whose dead lie also
in a living tomb of everlasting remembrance.

Let us remember those who came back;
those whose lives still bear the scars of war;
those who lost sight or limbs or reason;
those who lost faith in God
and hope for humanity.

Let us remember the continuing grace of God,
whose love holds all souls in life,
and to whom none is dead
but all are alive for ever.

6 THE TRYST

The minister says
They shall grow not old,
as we that are left grow old;
Age shall not weary them,
nor the years condemn.
At the going down of the sun
and in the morning,
We will remember them.

All   **We will remember them.**

[7 THE LAST POST]

[8 LAMENT]

9 THE SILENCE

Silence is kept for two minutes.

[10 REVEILLE]

11 PRAYER

The minister says
> In memory of those who died,
> may we be better men and women;
> and in gratitude to God,
> may we live as those who are not their own
> but who are bought with a price.

All **Amen.**

12 HYMN

13 OLD TESTAMENT LESSON

14 PSALM

15 NEW TESTAMENT LESSONS

16 APOSTLES' CREED

17 HYMN

18 SERMON

19 OFFERING

The minister says

Let us pray.

God of power and love,
bless our country and commonwealth.
Give wisdom and strength to the Queen,
govern those who make the laws,
guide those who direct our common life,
and grant that together we may fulfil our service
for the welfare of the whole people
and for your praise and glory.

Bless all members of the armed forces.
Defend them in danger.

Give them courage to meet
all occasions with discipline and loyalty.
So may they serve the cause of justice and peace,
to the honour of your name.

Bless our young people.
May they never see the flames of war,
or know the depths of cruelty
to which men and women can sink.
Grant that in their generation
they may be faithful soldiers
and servants of Jesus Christ.

Bless our friends
and those who were our enemies,
who suffered or are still suffering from war.
Grant that your love
may reach out to the wounded,
the disabled, the mentally distressed,
and those whose faith has been shaken
by what they have seen and endured.
Comfort all who mourn the death of loved ones,
and all who this day
miss the comradeship of friends.

Bless those who are homeless,
those who are refugees,
those who are hungry,
those who have lost their livelihood or security.
Help us to pledge ourselves
to comfort, support, and encourage others,
that all may live in a world
where evil and poverty are done away
and where human life
reflects the radiance of your kingdom.

Bless those in authority in every land,
and give them wisdom to know and courage to do
what is right.
Encourage those who work for peace,
who strive to improve international relations,
who seek new ways of reconciling
people of different race, colour, and creed.

Bless your Church throughout the world.
By your Holy Spirit,
draw the scattered flock of Christ into a visible unity,
and make your Church a sign of hope to our divided world.
Grant that we who bear your Son's name
may be instruments of your peace,
bringing peace to our homes,
our nation, and our world.

And now, rejoicing in the communion of saints,
we remember those whom you have gathered
from the storm of war into the peace of your presence,
and give you thanks for those whom we have known,
whose memory we treasure.
May the example of their devotion inspire us,
that we may be taught to live by those who learned to die.
And at the last, grant that we, being faithful till death,
may receive with them the crown of life that never fades;
through Jesus Christ our Lord.

All **Amen.**

All **Our Father ...**

21 HYMN

22 NATIONAL ANTHEM

23 BLESSING

> *The minister says*
> Let us pray.
>
> God grant to the living, grace;
> to the departed, rest;
> to the Church, the Queen, the Commonwealth, and all people,
>   peace and concord;
> and to us and all his servants
> life everlasting;
> and the blessing of God almighty,
> Father, Son, and Holy Spirit,
> be with you all.

All   **Amen.**

Scripture Lessons may be chosen from the following:

Old Testament
> *2 Samuel 23.13—17*
> *Isaiah 2.1—5*
> *Isaiah 25.1—9*
> *Isaiah 26.1—4*
> *Micah 4.1—5*

Epistle
> *Romans 8.31—39*
> *Ephesians 4.25 — 5.2*
> *Ephesians 6.10—18*
> *Revelation 21.1—7*

Gospel
> *Matthew 5.1—12*
> *John 15.9—17*

ORDER OF SERVICE FOR REMEMBRANCE SUNDAY 2005

as published by Churches Together in Britain and Ireland

GATHERING

All gather in silence

The presiding minister reads one or more of the following sentences
> God is our refuge and strength;
> a very present help in trouble.

Psalm 46.1

> I lift up my eyes to the hills —
> from whence will my help come?
> My help comes from the Lord,
> Who made heaven and earth.

Psalm 121.1,2

> This I call to mind,
> and therefore I have hope:
> the steadfast love of the Lord never ceases,
> his mercies never come to an end;
> they are new every morning.

Lamentations 3.21–23

> Those who wait for the Lord shall renew their strength,
> they shall mount up with wings like eagles,
> they shall run and not be weary
> they shall walk and not faint.

Isaiah 40.31

> What does the Lord require of you
> but to do justice, and to love kindness,
> and to walk humbly with your God?

Micah 6.8

The presiding minister continues
> We meet in the presence of God.

> We commit ourselves to work
> in penitence and faith
> for reconciliation between the nations,
> that all people may, together,
> live in freedom, justice and peace.

> We pray for all
> who in bereavement, disability and pain
> continue to suffer the consequences of fighting and terror.

> We remember with thanksgiving and sorrow
> those whose lives,
> in world wars and conflicts past and present,
> have been given and taken away.

REMEMBERING

An older person says
> They shall grow not old,
> as we that are left grow old;
> age shall not weary them,
> nor the years condemn.

A younger person may reply
> At the going down of the sun
> and in the morning,
> we will remember them.

All affirm
All **We will remember them.**

The beginning of the two-minute silence may be signalled

Silence

The completion of the silence may be signalled

The following prayer is said

> Ever-living God
> we remember those whom you have gathered
> from the storm of war into the peace of your presence;
> may that same peace
> calm our fears,
> bring justice to all peoples
> and establish harmony among the nations,
> through Jesus Christ our Lord.

All **Amen.**

The following hymn, or another that similarly expresses hope in God and trust for the future, may be sung

> **O God, our help in ages past,**
> **our hope for years to come,**
> **our shelter from the stormy blast,**
> **and our eternal home;**
>
> **Beneath the shadow of thy throne**
> **thy saints have dwelt secure;**
> **sufficient is thine arm alone,**
> **and our defence is sure.**
>
> **Before the hills in order stood,**
> **or earth received her frame,**
> **from everlasting thou art God,**
> **to endless years the same.**
>
> **A thousand ages in thy sight**
> **are like an evening gone;**
> **short as the watch that ends the night**
> **before the rising sun.**
>
> **Time, like an ever-rolling stream,**
> **bears all our years away;**
> **they fly forgotten, as a dream**
> **dies at the opening day.**
>
> **O God, our help in ages past,**
> **our hope for years to come,**
> **be thou our guard while troubles last,**
> **and our eternal home.**

The reader says

    Hear these words from the New Testament.

Either one or more of the following are read

    Peace I leave with you; my peace I give to you.
    I do not give to you as the world gives.
    Do not let your hearts be troubled,
    and do not let them be afraid.

John 14.27

    [No one has greater love than this,
    to lay down one's life for one's friends.

John 15.13, added to official text]

    The wisdom from above is first pure,
    then peaceable, gentle, willing to yield,
    full of mercy and good fruits,
    without a trace of partiality or hypocrisy.
    And a harvest of righteousness is sown in peace
    for those who make peace.

James 3.17–18

    This is the message we have heard from him
    and proclaim to you,
    that God is light
    and in him there is no darkness at all.

1 John 1.5

or the following is read

    When Jesus saw the crowds, he went up the mountain; and after he
    sat down, his disciples came to him. Then he began to speak, and
    taught them, saying:
        'Blessed are the poor in spirit,
            for theirs is the kingdom of heaven.
        Blessed are those who mourn,
            for they will be comforted.
        Blessed are the meek,
            for they will inherit the earth.
        Blessed are those who hunger and thirst for righteousness,
            for they will be filled.

Blessed are the merciful,
    for they will receive mercy.
Blessed are the pure in heart,
    for they will see God.
Blessed are the peacemakers,
    for they will be called children of God.
Blessed are those who are persecuted for righteousness' sake,
    for theirs is the kingdom of heaven.
'Blessed are you when people revile you and persecute you and utter all kinds of evil against you falsely on my account. Rejoice and be glad, for your reward is great in heaven, for in the same way they persecuted the prophets who were before you.'

Matthew 5.1–12

PRAYING TOGETHER

Prayer is led using either form of intercession below.

Let us pray for all who suffer as a result of conflict,
and ask that God may give us peace:

for the service men and women who have died in the violence of war,
each one remembered by and known to God;

May God give peace

All **God give peace.**

for those who love them in death as in life,
offering the distress of our grief and the sadness of our loss;

May God give peace

All **God give peace.**

for all members of the armed forces who are in danger this day,
remembering family, friends and all who pray for their safe return;

May God give peace

All **God give peace.**

for civilian women, children and men
whose lives are disfigured by war or terror,
calling to mind in penitence the anger and hatreds of humanity;

May God give peace

All **God give peace.**

for peace-makers and peace-keepers,
who seek to keep this world secure and free;

May God give peace
All **God give peace.**

for all who bear the burden and privilege of leadership,
political, military and religious;
asking for gifts of wisdom and resolve
in the search for reconciliation and peace.

May God give peace
All **God give peace.**

O God of truth and justice,
we hold before you those whose memory we cherish,
and those whose names we will never know.
Help us to lift our eyes above the torment of this broken world,
and grant us the grace to pray for those who wish us harm.
As we honour the past, may we put our faith in your future;
for you are the source of life and hope, now and for ever.
All **Amen.**

Or else this form of intercession may be used

In peace let us pray to the Lord.

We pray for the leaders of the nations,
that you will guide them in the ways of freedom, justice and truth.
Lord, in your mercy
All **hear our prayer.**

We pray for those who bear arms on behalf of the nation,
that they may have discipline and discernment,
  courage and compassion.
Lord, in your mercy
All **hear our prayer.**

We pray for our enemies, and those who wish us harm,
that you may turn the hearts of all to kindness and friendship.
Lord, in your mercy
All **hear our prayer.**

We pray for the wounded and the captive,
the grieving and the homeless,
that in all their trials they may know your love and support.
Lord, in your mercy

All **hear our prayer.**

Most Holy God and Father,
hear our prayers for all who strive for peace,
and all who yearn for justice.
Help us, who today remember the cost of war,
to work for a better tomorrow;
and, as we commend to you lives lost in terror and conflict,
bring us all, in the end, to the peace of your presence;
through Christ our Lord.
Amen.

All join together in the Lord's Prayer

All **Our Father, who art in heaven,**
hallowed be thy name;
thy kingdom come;
thy will be done;
on earth as it is in heaven.
Give us this day our daily bread.
And forgive us our trespasses,
as we forgive those who trespass against us.
And lead us not into temptation;
but deliver us from evil.
For thine is the kingdom,
the power and the glory,
for ever and ever.
Amen.

RESPONDING IN HOPE AND COMMITMENT

Representative and other members of the public come forward to lay wreaths, light candles or offer other symbols of remembrance and hope, such as single flowers or crosses.

The Kohima Epitaph is said
> When you go home tell them of us and say:
> 'for your tomorrow, we gave our today.'

A hymn may be sung.

The act of commitment is made
> Let us commit ourselves to responsible living and faithful service.
>
> Will you strive for all that makes for peace?

All **We will.**

> Will you seek to heal the wounds of war?

All **We will.**

> Will you work for a just future for all humanity?

All **We will.**

> Merciful God,
> we offer to you the fears in us
> that have not yet been cast out by love:
> May we accept the hope you have placed
> in the hearts of all people,
> and live lives of justice, courage and mercy;
> through Jesus Christ our risen Redeemer.

All **Amen.**

The National Anthem(s) are sung.

The following blessing is used

>God grant to the living, grace,
>to the departed, rest,
>to the Church, the Queen, the Commonwealth, and all people,
>[*or* to the Church, the State, and all people,][†]
>>unity, peace and concord,
>and to us and all God's servants, life everlasting;
>
>and the blessing of God almighty,
>Father, Son and Holy Spirit
>be with you all
>and remain with you always.

All **Amen.**

[†] *The form in parenthesis is appropriate for use in the Republic of Ireland and other territories outside the dominion of the Crown.*

This order then reprints the Act of Penitence, the Act of Commitment and the prayer after the silence from the 1968 order together with an alternative intercession which, in this booklet, is included in the main text.

The 2005 Order of Service, published by Churches Together in Britain and Ireland, may be freely reproduced.

REMEMBRANCE RESOURCES
from Common Worship: Times and Seasons

INTRODUCTION

[A Remembrance Sunday service, first commended for general use by the Archbishop of Canterbury, the Cardinal Archbishop of Westminster and the Moderator of the Free Church Federal Council in 1968 and revised in 1984, is widely available. See pages 108–15 above.]

The following supplementary resources are provided for use at Holy Communion, Morning or Evening Prayer or A Service of the Word.

INVITATION TO CONFESSION

> Let us confess to God the sins and shortcomings of the world;
> its pride, its selfishness, its greed;
> its evil divisions and hatreds.
> Let us confess our share in what is wrong,
> and our failure to seek and establish that peace
> which God wills for his children.

INTRODUCTION TO THE PEACE

> Jesus said: Peace I leave with you; my peace I give to you.
> I do not give to you as the world gives.

John 14.27

AN ACT OF REMEMBRANCE

> Let us remember before God,
> and commend to his safe keeping:
> those who have died for their country in war;
> [those whom we knew, and whose memory we treasure;]
> and all who have lived and died
> in the service of the peoples of the world.

A list of those to be remembered by name may then be read.

      They shall grow not old as we that are left grow old:
      Age shall not weary them, nor the years condemn.
      At the going down of the sun and in the morning
      We will remember them.

All   **We will remember them.**

      (The Last Post)   *The Silence*   *(The Reveille)*

      Almighty and eternal God,
      from whose love in Christ we cannot be parted,
      either by death or life:
      Hear our prayers and thanksgivings
      for all whom we remember this day;
      fulfil in them the purpose of your love;
      and bring us all, with them, to your eternal joy;
      through Jesus Christ our Lord.

All   **Amen.**

The Kohima Epitaph may be read
      When you go home tell them of us and say:
      'For your tomorrow, we gave our today.'

BLESSING

      God grant to the living, grace;
      to the departed, rest;
      to the Church, the Queen, the Commonwealth and all the world,
          peace and concord;
      and to us and all his servants, life everlasting;

      and the blessing of God almighty,
      the Father, the Son and the Holy Spirit
      be among you and remain with you always.

All   **Amen.**

God is our refuge and strength,
a very present help in trouble.

Psalm 46.1

Our help comes from the Lord,
the maker of heaven and earth.

cf Psalm 121.2

Blessed are the peacemakers,
for they will be called children of God.

Matthew 5.9

Jesus said, In the world you will face persecution.
But take courage; I have overcome the world.

John 16.33

MUSICAL RESOURCES

As recommended in the 2005 order

HYMNS

These hymns (listed alphabetically by first line) may be found in major hymnbooks such as Common Praise, New English Hymnal, Hymns and Psalms, Rejoice and Sing, Church Hymnary Fourth Edition, *and the various collections published by Mayhew.*

A mighty wind invades the world
Almighty Father, who for us thy Son didst give

Be still, my soul, the Lord is on your side

Christ is the world's true light

Eternal Father, strong to save

For the healing of the nations

God is our strength and refuge
God of freedom, God of justice
God with humanity made one
Great is thy faithfulness

Here from all nations

I, the Lord of Sea and Sky
In a world where people walk in darkness
In Christ there is no east or west
It is God who holds the nations

Jesus Christ is waiting
Jesus, Lord, we look to thee
Judge eternal, throned in splendour

Lead us, heavenly Father, lead us
Lord, for the years
Lord, save thy world; in bitter need

Now thank we all our God

O God of earth and altar
O God, our help in ages past

Peace, perfect peace
Pray for the Church, afflicted and oppressed
Praise, my soul, the King of heaven
Pray that Jerusalem may have peace and prosperity

Son of God, eternal Saviour

The kingdom of God is justice and joy
The right hand of God
Through the night of doubt and sorrow
Thy kingdom come, O God
To thee, O God, we fly

We pray for peace
We turn to you, O God of every nation
Will you come and follow me

In Timothy Dudley Smith: A House of Praise, *Oxford University Press / Hope Publishing* 2003

Behold, a broken world, we pray
Eternal God, before whose face we stand
            (specially written for Remembrancetide)
Remember, Lord, the world you made

In Common Ground: A Song Book for all the Churches, *St Andrew Press,* 1998

What shall we pray for those who have died
We lay our broken world in sorrow at your feet

SONGS

Kum ba yah, my Lord

Lead us from death to life
Let there be love shared among us
Let there be peace on earth

Make me a channel of your peace

O Lord, the clouds are gathering

Shalom, my friends

TAIZÉ CHANTS

Christ of compassion (In te confido)

Da pacem, Domine
Dona nobis pacem
Dona nobis pacem, Domine

In God alone

Jesus, remember me, when you come into your kingdom

O Lord, hear my prayer

OTHER MUSIC

The RSCM publishes a list of suitable choral anthems and organ music in Sunday by Sunday.
Details may be found at the RSCM website:
www.rscm.com / sundaybysunday

OTHER MUSICAL RESOURCES

Eternal Father

Here is a version of 'The Naval Hymn' for all three Services

Eternal Father, strong to save,
Whose arm doth bind the restless wave,
Who bid'st the mighty ocean deep
Its own appointed limits keep;
O hear us when we cry to thee,
for those in peril on the sea.

O Christ, the Universal Lord,
who suffered death by nails and sword,
from all assault of deadly foe
sustain thy soldiers where they go;
and evermore hold in thy hand
all those in peril on the land.

O Holy Spirit, Lord of grace,
Who fills with strength the human race,
Inspire us all to know the right;
Guide all who dare the eagle's flight;
And underneath thy wings of care
Guard all from peril in the air.

O Trinity of love and power!
Our brethren shield in danger's hour;
From rock and tempest, fire and foe,
Protect them wheresoe'er they go;
Thus evermore shall rise to thee,
Praise from the air, the land and sea.

verses 1,4: William Whiting (1825–78); verses 2,3: BE

This adaptation was made by the author in online consultation with members of 'Christians on the Internet' www.coin.org.uk

MUSIC FOR THE LAST POST AND THE REVEILLE

Last Post

Rouse / Reveille

The music for the 'Last Post' and the 'Reveille' is made available courtesy of the band of the Royal Electrical and Mechanical Engineers. It is in the public domain, and may be photocopied.